Facing Death Together

Facing Death Together

The Pastor and the Family

by

Kenneth E. Sullivan

Beacon Hill Press of Kansas City
Kansas City, Missouri

ISBN: 083-411-3236

Printed in the
United States of America

Cover: Royce Ratcliff

10   9   8   7   6   5   4   3   2   1

Dedicated
to the
memory of my mother
whose fight to live and drive to restore
were powerful factors in
weaving the threads of a broken family
into the fabric of love
to carry on through bereavement and fear
and rebuild a home

Contents

Foreword

In recommending a book to be read, one is also recommending a person, a spirit, and an action. Any attempt to write a book always throws one back upon the humiliating consciousness of his own insufficiency. But often the heart knows more than can ever be explained in words.

Over the years the author of *Facing Death Together: The Pastor and the Family* has served the church with quiet distinction and has had a keen awareness of the distresses of life crying out in the night. To endorse his book is to endorse the author's insight as he finds the answer in the mystery of faith and the obedience of love.

I recall coming into the celebrated "Cardboard Palace" on the campus of Eastern Nazarene College and being introduced to my new roommate. He accepted me with the same love and warmth that is reflected throughout his book. Years later, in my time of terrible personal loss, he crossed the country to share in my hurt and grief. Few people in the ENC connection over the years have been held in such high esteem.

I commend this book as it deals with the matter of death and grief in the family. The haunting and unanswered questions take in all of our lives, and you will sense the author's compassion reaching out to you as he journeys on through circumstances that are common to people in every parish.

Anyone passing through deep waters and sensing great need will find support and love in these shared personal experiences. The author's pastoral ministry and graduate studies qualify him to write on this theme of dealing with death and dying. Looking beyond his studies and passing through his own dark places is demonstration of his hope in a personal God we can trust—in hard places.

—ALEXANDER "SANDY" ARDREY

Acknowledgments

It is much more simple to write a book than it is to explain why you did it! And, indeed, it is much more difficult to acknowledge all who had a part in the making. Every effort in life involves many people, and we are all very much a part of each other's lives.

This book began as a research project on the pastor's role in dealing with the terminally ill patient and as a partial requirement for the master's degree in the class of pastoral counseling. It has been extended to embrace the wider commingling of the pastor and the family in working through the fears and anxieties of life. *Facing Death Together* encompasses the ministry of the pastor, the care for the family, and the answer in love at the Cross as it relates to death.

I owe a great debt to Dr. Edward S. Mann, a person strong in mind, natural in wisdom, penetrating in insight, and gifted with the ability to work through problems that confront and challenge. He stood by and encouraged me through many difficulties as he urged this publication.

Intellectual and spiritual vigor, with a strong and tender touch of humanity, exemplifies Dr. Cecil Paul, under whose influence this work began. The magic of encouragement was in every phase of his classroom, and his teaching was held in its power. He allowed me to share in this setting.

Thanks to Jean Sullivan, secretary of the Division of Graduate Studies, who typed, argued, and encouraged. Her wit, love, and concern brought us through many rugged days.

To the ones who said, "You can't!" when I thought I could—thank you for the challenge.

To the ones who said, "You can!" when I was sure I could not—thank you for the courage.

To the ones who left my office when I tried to impress them with my manuscript, and the ones who stayed and listened—thank you for the confidence.

To all who criticized, encouraged, or helped in any way, I owe a debt of love and appreciation.

Introduction

"Why . . . ?"

"Because!"

"Because why?"

Many times as a child, I stood before the judgment seat of an irate stepfather, facing his seemingly unanswerable questions.

"Why were you late getting home from school?"

"Why didn't you finish your chores as you were supposed to?"

"Why did you do what you did?"—whatever it happened to be.

My answer, which I knew would be inadequate, was usually, "Because." His inevitable follow-up was always, "Because why?" How often I stood before him, searching desperately for a reasonable answer! But, try as I might, I don't think I was ever able to produce a "because" that would satisfy his "why?"

This scene extends itself throughout our lives and becomes especially significant in the relationship between a pastor and his people. As pastors, we may live in fear of facing questions for which we have no satisfying reply. And we can go to great lengths searching for answers to protect our inadequacies. We forget that laypersons want us to talk to them simply in the plain and common language of earth. Great answers are simple answers and are rarely found in the genius of the pastor.

Nowhere is the confusion more acute than in the death scene. The grieving heart is always asking, "Why . . . ?" and is looking for an answer more fulfilling than the "because" that we supply in our attempt to satisfy its probing. Around these two words hover the great perplexities of the suffering person as he continues to search for answers in his confrontation with death. Grief finds its greatest anticipation and least satisfaction in this distressing encounter with the "why" and the "because" that engulf every crisis.

In facing life's great problems, we, as helpers, look for standardized answers to satisfy our own demands for adequacy. Often we forget that our answers must satisfy the grieving person as well. In spite of our quest for personal satisfaction, it is imperative that we extend an abundance of understanding and empathy to those who are grieving. As pastors, we may encounter convictions and patterns of belief that do not conform to our well-structured standards. In a guarded attempt to cope, we can very easily block out inquiry and damage credibility with respect to the crying issues of the person who stands in need of understanding. The danger is that in our eager search for rational answers we leave the one who has the deepest need in confusion.

I cannot forget the words of a lonely husband as we visited the graveside of his wife one year after her death. The flowers had faded, and the brown soil had turned green with new grass, but his heart had failed to mend. He turned to me and said, "Preacher, we have found a remedy for everything else, but the heart goes on hurting." And the truth is that this need does grow greater and the heart does keep on hurting as our society grows in self-sufficiency in every other area.

Our world is full of grieving and fearful people from every facet of life who are searching for a better "because" than we seem to be able to provide for them. We will need a great deal of insight as we endeavor to minister to grieving families in every level of society.

1

The Problem: Grief and Fear of Death

The pastor holds a vital position as he stands between two extremes in the routine of living. One side is marked by a sense of permanence, stability, and confidence in the on-goingness of life. The other erupts in insecurity, imbalance, and anxiety as the flow of life is broken by the threat of death. In the center of this situation the pastor stands with the one who has been torn by the intrusion as they reach up together for an affirmation greater than the circumstances.

A distraught father called me at two o'clock one morning, and I listened while he tried, between sobs, to tell me about a car accident that he was certain had claimed the life of his only son. As we stood together in the accident room of the hospital, hoping and praying for the best but fearing the worst, he said to me, "Nothing like this has ever happened to our family before." His sky had suddenly blackened by one fatal night, and out of the depths of that darkness we tried to reach out together for some small ray of light and hope.

I am not a professional counselor, but in my pastoral encounters I have been constantly aware of a deep cry of distress resident in the heart of the sufferer. My journey through life has taken me down into the valley where death has been as much a part of life as the living itself. It was the custom in our rural community to hang black crepe on the doorknob to tell all who passed by that death had just visited the home. This colored my earliest memories as I grew up amid superstition, fear, anger, and mental anxieties, without the benefit or solace of a caring minister or counselor. Ironically I found myself in the position of a pastor reaching for that doorknob draped in sorrow. I have learned that every family has its own sorrow and is reaching out through pain for sympathy and some recognition of its tears.

The word *death* has taken on new meaning as people try to cope with the termination of life as we know it. Death does not always come enshrouded immediately in grief. To many people today, death has lost its cloak of awesomeness. In a society where so much leisure time is spent pursuing pleasure, we often fail to consider consequences until they happen to us. Most people view death as something inevitable— sooner or later they will face it. They try to push the event into the distant future to worry about when the crisis comes. A few people (especially young TV watchers) view death merely as a shot from a gun, a stab with a switchblade, or a trip to Boot Hill. They don't consider the trauma of intricate family relationships, the funeral with its consequences, and the broken dreams. Almost no one looks at death as an immediate possibility or is prepared to cope with it when it comes. Few people seem to be perturbed by the thought that within the next 100 years all those now living on the earth will be dead. We have learned to ignore the threat of death and its consequence on our well-being.

Ernest Becker (1973) writes, "The idea of death, the fear of it, haunts the human animal like nothing else; it is a mainspring of human activity—activity designed largely to avoid the fatality of death, to overcome it by denying it some way, is the final destiny of man." He goes further to compare other cultures that face death with great rejoicing and festivities and see it as an ultimate promotion. But Becker adds, "The

Westerners have trouble believing this anymore, which is what makes the fear of death so prominent a part of our psychological makeup."

Our fear of death seems to be exaggerated when we are aware of its coming. Somewhere deep within us we have erected barriers that strongly affirm, "It will never happen to me." This is especially true when death announces its coming with a precise date, predicts the method of its arrival, and provides little preparation for its acceptance. Often it brings fear to the recipient that is not dispelled until the day death arrives.

How do we respond when the sentence of death has been pronounced with a definite date and where an appeal for an extension of time does not lie within the jurisdiction of one's desire to live? There is an inborn security bound up in all of us that will not allow us to assent blindly to this sort of pronouncement. We struggle to lay hold on every bit of hope available, even to plead favoritism with our Maker. The declaration of impending death will precipitate grief in an entire family. In an effort to accept the truth and deal with their overwhelming grief, families need all the stabilizing resources available.

In the pages that follow we will investigate grief and the role of the minister in the death scene. The person-in-dilemma holds the most important role in the drama, while the responsibility of helper in dealing with the family as well as the patient is thrust upon the minister. The pastor does not come on the scene as a creative genius, nor is he probing deeply for impossible answers. Often he stands speechless before the waiting family with words that only the heart can hold. But he is there nonetheless! And his greatest reason for being there is as a care provider and a resource person for spiritual strength in this crisis of adjustment from life into death.

In an epilogue I share a personal experience in which I am the person-in-dilemma. Utterances and expressions of grief that none but God could hear and understand are taken from a day-by-day encounter with affliction in the struggle for meaning.

In conclusion, we offer some prayers for those who may be in sorrow and suffering and are reaching out to God for consolation.

2

The Personal

I was born in the shadow of the coffin, surrounded by Irish custom and superstition. There was never any question as to how much was real and how much was fantasy in this life-style. Since childhood knows no determining factor for sifting out authenticity, I accepted it as a normal way of life. The channels through which superstition ran were cut deeper with each passing generation, and no one felt a moral obligation to investigate. The existence of unseen forces at work to destroy us was never an issue, but rather, when and how they would be expressed. When the wind whistled through the rafters of the old wooden farmhouse, and pots and pans were set out to catch the raindrops through the leaky roof, every sound was monitored, and every raindrop told its own story. The creaking boards and the sounds from the barn with each clap of thunder measured the calamity that was sure to strike. Each storm was compared in destruction to the previous one, while we hovered together in the kitchen, waiting for morning to come. Even the moonlit nights were marked for the length and direction of the shadows they cast.

One night lightning struck a large hackmatack tree in our neighbor's yard. It split the tree from top to bottom, carefully making its way around each limb and leaving a round hole in the road bank where it escaped. We spent all summer looking for the "thunderbolt" that our neighbor warned us would return to strike again if not located and destroyed. I never knew if he really believed this or not, but it kept us in fear, as we were certain that some other home would be the victim if we failed in our search.

In the midst of this superstitious background one of my earliest memories rests in the middle of a wake for a great-uncle who had died an untimely death. Some of the details probably would not be so vivid had I not heard them re-counted on numerous occasions by my grandmother. How-ever, nothing about the occasion was artificial, but the cir-cumstances of the moment had to fulfill the tradition by which he had lived and honor the custom by which he was to be buried. So the family removed my great-uncle from the crude coffin and stood him, stiff and cold, in the corner of the parlor where a bottle of rum was placed under his arm and a clay pipe forced between his teeth. The atmosphere was charged with elation while drinking and dancing were high-lighted against the background of professional keening. In the midst of the celebration, a man in black entered the room out of the darkness, and everything became still. He spoke in low tones to the family and said strange words as he fondled some beads in his hands, as well as some other religious arti-cles. After sprinkling water about the room and making the sign of the cross before my great-uncle, he went out again into the night. I learned later that this represented the release of the loved one with the good wishes of the family and the blessings of the church. It also concluded the role of the min-istering servant to the family until the day of the funeral and the burial of the loved one. But the keening struck terror to my heart! Terror that lingered long after the mourning had ceased.

Out of this experience and the circumstances to follow,

there began a long process of learning, misunderstanding, and pain. Even though a child's mind has a resistance to reality and all of its ramifications, I lived in an environment that nurtured uneasiness, anxiety, and fear.

At the age of four years, too young to grasp the significance of life and death, I found myself beside the deathbed of my father. I knew something dreadful was taking place because my grandmother began to make the same sounds she had made at the wake of my great-uncle. Since disaster had moved in on the wings of death, the doors and windows of the room were flung open, and she began to beat the air with her apron to get rid of the evil spirits.

Then the doors were closed, and the family began to cry. Some men of the community came in to "lay out the corpse," and a man with a black horse and black covered wagon came in with a big box. And we stood around and watched as they put my father in it. Then everybody went away, except us. The big box with my father in it stood in the middle of the parlor floor, resting on some crude sawhorses, for several days and nights, and every night people came in to keen and to celebrate. And one night a lady picked me up in her arms and said, "Take a good look at your father so that you will never forget him." (Her insight was remarkable, because the memory of that ashen face is stamped indelibly on my mind.) And she said, "God has taken your father away." It all jumbled in my mind, and I wondered why God, whoever He was, would take my father away. I was confused. Then one day the man with the black horse and the black covered wagon came back again, and he said some words to us about something while everybody kept quiet. My mother began to cry while she held us tightly in her arms. They put a cover on the box and took it away with my father in it, and the man in black followed it out to the wagon. They never came back, and I never saw my father again!

There was something fearsome and mysterious about this whole drama, as the family tried so hard to evade death but was forced to embrace the event that is so uncontrollable and so far-reaching in its power.

An important lesson I learned from my mother is that the ability to reconstruct, along with the drive to live, is a powerful force in gathering the resources of an individual together to carry on through pain and despair. After the death of my father an outside bonfire was built on the shore of the lake to burn the death clothes and to boil water for the housecleaning. My mother slipped and fell into the fire and lay in bed for several months, hovering between life and death from burns over her entire body. Neighbors came to look on and to prescribe remedies for her recovery while predicting her imminent demise, based on similar mishaps in their own families. In the evening friends gathered around her bed and in the eerie kerosene lamplight recounted experiences of death notices, warnings, and forerunners that had accompanied tragedies in this small community. They listened for sounds and happenings that would herald the coming of the death angel. It was a marked community where we lived, and only the winds knew where and when the next visitation of doom would fall.

I sat on my grandmother's lap, wrapped snugly in her apron, while she rocked in the big chair and took her turn interpreting the various sounds that broke the silence of the night. I did not understand what was happening, but I wondered if God was getting ready to take away my mother as He had taken my father. I was frightened; and when I tried to sleep at night, I would see ugly faces staring at me and hear strange sounds about my head. I was sure that getting out from under my grandmother's apron was to court disaster. I learned that darkness breeds trouble and that death was dreadfully attached to every noise of the night. Then one day

22

my mother told me that God had let her live so that she could make a home for her four fatherless children. I still could not understand it all, but I was glad that God's anger had for some reason turned into compassion and that He was going to let me keep my mother. There was no minister available to help my family understand that death and dying are an intrinsic part of life.

My mother desperately clung to hope, which she reinforced with a great amount of love for her family. Yet it seemed almost like a normal course of events the day that my little brother was killed by a neighbor's pulp truck and delivered, without warning, into my mother's arms as she came to answer a knock at the door. Very little time transpired before the scene was repeated—a house full of friends who came to comfort, to keen, and to lay out the corpse. My mother cried all night, and the atmosphere was charged with fear and trepidation. Again I saw God as an angry intruder. But I remember one well-meaning member of our neighborhood putting her arms around Mother and saying, "Well, Ella, God knows best!" And I got mad at God all over again! I could not understand why He was taking everybody away.

I went with my stepfather to the minister's home to make arrangements for the funeral for my brother. On the way home in the horse and buggy I asked him why God had taken my brother away. His "because" was an embarrassed effort to dismiss and ignore God, based, I suppose, on a lack of religious commitment on his part. He could not satisfy my "why."

Our family struggled on in the acceptance of these tragic events, and we had no religious leader to comfort us with a message from a loving and caring Heavenly Father. When the pronouncement was given to us by the local doctor that my sister had six months to live, my vindictive judgment toward God and His interference in our family again became very severe. The rebellion and anger that filled my heart lingered long after the day she died. I do not believe at that time it could have been reconciled by any message of love that acknowledged and trusted God, however great He might be!

Several years later the message of a loving God, through the gift unto death of His own Son, changed my outlook and brought me to an acceptance of His will and ways. The fellowship of suffering, I discovered, was to include God rather than keep Him on the outside as a perpetrator of pain and despair.

When my stepfather died, another human relationship was broken, but this time it did not pose a threat to my faith in God and His gospel of love. However, I was quite unprepared for the experience that was to plummet the family into its first real encounter with ministerial benefit.

The structure of our life-style had begun to change as the family became more church related; however, the services of the minister were limited to times of dire necessity. Since my stepfather adhered to one denominational preference and my mother subscribed to another, we had two ministers vying for top billing at his funeral. My mother invited her minister to have the sermon at the service. The prayer, being the second big item for the occasion, was passed to the other minister to perform. No bridge could span the chasm that opened when my mother was informed by my stepfather's minister of this breach of ministerial etiquette, as he contended that he should have had the honor of preaching the funeral sermon. Since the prayer preceded the sermon, the minister took advantage of the moment in an attempt to gain back his honor and spent 25 minutes on his knees before the open coffin in a scathing diatribe against the other minister's doctrine. He used my mother as a prime example of its adherents. The amount of liberty that should be taken with a family in grief did not seem to concern either man. My mother's minister turned the sermon into a 30-minute defense of his doctrine, giving every opponent a berth in eternal perdition.

Then came the long ride to the cemetery for the burial on that cold January afternoon. The two ministers rode together in the same vehicle, and such a heated argument ensued on the way that they were unaware of having passed the burying ground until they were 10 miles down the old country road. We were left standing at the graveside another 30 minutes until the men of comfort and compassion returned to complete their mission of mercy. And only one of the ministers came to the graveside for the final rites.

My ideas of the role of the minister in dealing with a family in crisis were formulating. I was searching for some order of love and understanding in an hour of need and desperation. But the anger and protest we had witnessed were a bit perplexing, and I was convinced that there must be a better way to minister to a grieving and mourning family.

Following this scene, our family was soon thrust into the normal aunt, uncle, grandparent, and neighbor death as time weeded out the aged and visited the homes of the unsuspecting. The front room continued as the funeral parlor, and neighbors stood around to gossip and to predict. Unusual and frightening experiences were recounted at every occasion as death, fear, and fantasy mingled with reality.

Then came World War II and the check-off list in the flight room each morning after the night raids, with the red markers beside the names of the buddies who did not come back. Few homes escaped the dreaded ringing of the doorbell and the telegram; a man in uniform with somber voice began the chilling obituary: "I'm sorry to inform you that . . ."

When I first sensed a divine call into the pastoral ministry, I questioned the wisdom and justice of God as well as His sense of humor. Some of my best friends were critical of my decision. I was often reminded that perfect love casts out fear, that commitment covers anxiety, and that a true child of God is not enslaved by the past. I agreed with them in principle as I carried on through superstition and pain and fear with the scars of my childhood training ever present.

Being reared in all the superstition of the country background, fear was part of everyday living. You walked the roads at night in great dread, and you ran past the cemetery with a distorted sense of destiny. You passed a church in double time after a recent funeral where the lingerings of the dead remained long after the tears of mourning ceased to flow. I discovered that it requires many encounters with God and constant searching for His love to free oneself from the past.

It did not take me too long to discover a uniformity in life's circumstances as I began to minister. In the first few months of my ministerial duties there was an encounter with two murders; a wait in the courtroom to hear the judge in black robe pass the death sentence on a 17-year-old boy; an attempt to minister to a mother and her son waiting trial for allegedly having shot a drunken husband and father; a fight to possess a corpse from a court of justice before the feuding families could mete out more bloodshed and retribution; and a question from a distraught father as we stood beside the little white coffin: "Why did God take my baby?" I found it easier on the other side of the table!

It seems that all through one's ministry there is an interplay of the human and the divine. To be able to harmonize the two into a viable working relationship is the final goal, and often the struggle, of the minister.

Combining the experiences of the past with hope for the future puts one in a position of constant evaluation of the unfolding present, and often the judgment is severe. This was brought into focus early in my ministry. I made a dramatic effort to overcome the human, hoping for divine intervention, which took a leave of absence in the crisis.

No seminary training, however valid, prepares one adequately for the real-life experiences that lurk in the dark shadows of reality. I was conducting my first funeral—alone—in the small front living room of the deceased. It was a private funeral with the immediate family only in attendance. The man who held the highest office in his denomination was present as the sole surviving brother. He also represented the more dignified, less compassionate, and most formal form of worship in the church. His stern eyes, which shut out any semblance of empathy, were glued to every move that I made. His black robes and white clerical collar added reverential fear as if he had just come in out of the night. There were four others present, two of whom were mentally deranged.

My congregation of five living souls was in front of me, as well as the lectern on which rested my Bible and copious quantities of notes, ready to be delivered to this mourning family. The coffin, directly behind me, was resting in the bay window niche of this crowded room. As I finished reading a challenging passage from Paul and stepped back to impress my confrere with an extemporaneous prayer, I backed against the coffin. Immediately my years on Grandmother's lap came to preserve and to protect—I knew the hand of the corpse had reached for me! In lunging forward to escape the inevitable, I knocked over the lectern and fell with it into the lap of the sole surviving brother. He did not move, and he did not smile, nor did he show any sign of emotion either to condemn or to sympathize. Alone, I picked up the lectern, gathered up my Bible and my notes and poetry about "crossing the bar" and "one clear call for me," and proceeded with my discourse on "If a man die, shall he live again?" (Job 14:14).

When the ordeal was finally over, out in the cold cemetery, no one voiced appreciation for the message or allowed that any words of comfort had been given or received. The mourning family walked to their cars and returned home. I walked to mine.

3

The Person in Pain

The problems and procedures of living out the various aspects of one's life must be carried out within a time span of threescore and 10 years, a little more or a little less. Ambitions and commitments are encompassed in this brief allotment of time. When this is thwarted by illness or a lingering disease, there is a further reaching out for an answer that must be defined for the circumstances.

Often I visited an elderly lady who had been bedridden for over 15 years. Her tiny body was twisted, her arms and hands were misshapen, and her head rested heavily on her chest from years of arthritic pain. One day while sympathizing with her about her suffering, she looked up at me the best she could and through much pain pointed to a low-hanging motto on her wall: "What time I am afraid, I will trust in thee" (Ps. 56:3). She had already discovered something that I, as helper, had failed to provide. But it is within this framework that every person must find purpose and meaning in life, which is usually a process of sharing relations with others.

This sharing process in life is necessary for the growth of the person. It is also within this process of living that another dimension enters when the person, sooner or later, faces the experience of death. We take a stand beside the person for this interruption of life in an attempt to share in the protests and approvals as death works its way into the family life-style.

The matters of concern in the problems of death quickly resolve themselves into two vital issues—to help the patient approach it without fear and hopefully with a confident faith in God and to ease the emotional stress of the grieving. A sense of security and a reaching out to be rescued highlights the need for the person as well as for the family. In the mystery of death there is always a point that can never be touched, yet there is always hope, through prayer, to a still broader glory. In death, as in grief, the comforting presence of the minister can be a major factor in leading one through the crisis to this hope.

The call for help may come at any time of the day or night. But neither the inopportune time nor any lofty position of the pastor must ever destroy the sacred trust that has been placed in him, for he goes out as a helper and a representative of Jesus Christ to the place of sorrow and suffering. We are servants of one another, and to chafe under the opportunity, no matter how inconvenient, is to destroy confidence and often trust in God.

How shocking is the news of impending death! No matter how prudently the message has been delivered, it always comes wrapped in black. Sometimes it seems wise for the family doctor to expose his diagnosis to the patient in company with other members of the family. Often the burden rests with the minister to share the probabilities, especially if there have been close ties with the family in a church relationship. Hopefully, it will not come as a message of doom through some impersonal source, endangering family confidence and ministerial trust.

In whatever manner the news comes, hope suffers a hefty blow. Often there is faith in God to cushion the full force of reality. Even if this faith is absent, a will to live seems to be inherent in all people for such periods of distress. In spite of all the help, external or internal, there comes with the pronouncement an overpowering sense of aloneness. In the days, months, or even years of being dependent on others, death still remains a personal thing. Every person does his own dying.

Joseph W. Matthews (1964) speaks about death as a "powerful, individual happening." In amplifying his observation by some personal experiences, he says:

> I remember during the war I wanted to help men die. I was never fully able to do this. I tried. Sometimes I placed a cigarette in a soldier's mouth as we talked. Sometimes I quoted for him the Twenty-third Psalm. Sometimes I wiped the sweat and blood from his face. Sometimes I held his hand. Sometimes I did nothing. It was a rude shock to discover that I could not, in the final sense, help a man to die. Each had to do his own dying, alone.

Unless a person has been laid at the doorstep of death, the force of this statement is reduced to mere terminology without much sense of reality. But when the knock has sounded at your door and the burden has been left for you to handle, the personal aspect becomes overwhelming.

It was Sunday afternoon in the cemetery at Bill's funeral. I had been with him through his suffering. I had knelt beside him at the camp meeting healing service. I had visited him in the hospital on a daily basis. I stood by his bedside with the family as we watched him die. How helpless to see a friend and loved one slip beyond our grasp! We could not help.

Now, during his committal, I was stricken with a severe heart attack and woke up three days later in the hospital. This was followed by complications with medication and malfunctioning kidneys, and recovery seemed to be slipping from my grasp. A sense of urgency was building up in the room as the attendants rushed about with their professional duties. The attending nurse was also a fellow minister with whom I had been associated in a chaplaincy program at the state hospital in the city. Together with the doctor, he shared with me the seriousness of my condition and informed me of the grave possibility of my own death before morning if certain conditions persisted.

I wanted to reach out for something, but everything began to slip away. I heard words, but they did not register any meaning to me. I saw people, but they were statues. The time for getting, being, and doing was over. The finality was very real!

How quickly hope degenerates into despair. Until this point I had been recovering. Now I was dying. I was no longer standing beside Bill's bed, for the role had taken a reverse turn, and the message of the visitation of death was being passed to me. I was on the couch, and I was alone. No amount of comforting, counseling, or consoling was necessary or desired—it was a unique experience, and it was personal. In those next few hours I walked down through that dark valley of death all by myself—it could not be shared. Even though I survived and my sentence has been postponed, I learned that death is a journey into eternity that has to be taken all by oneself.

In spite of the disheartening aspects of death, one always leaves the door of life open for a possible delay. Hope is the last ally to loosen its grip. Life has a way of shooting its darts through death's strong armor. This is true in the deepest spiritual sense, for when one is reaching out for hope, he is reaching out for God. The groping takes the form of prayer, and praying at the moment of death is a prayer of trust and hope. Kubler-Ross comments:

> We must learn to die in order that we may learn to live, that growing to be who you truly are requires some

times that you die to the life chosen for you by society, that each new step of growth involves a throwing off of the shackles restraining you . . . in order to grow, you must continually die and be reborn *(1969, 147)*.

She continues: "When the things we value most in life are destroyed, we can respond in several ways" and explains that a person can go into a life of depressed feelings or try to conceal the fact of death from one's consciousness. Sometimes people give themselves wholeheartedly to creative relationships with others. She concludes, "Becoming open to other people and remaining open to them is more easily said than done" (150).

So, in the necessary struggle for a new identity as we approach death, high value is placed upon relationships with others on the one hand and the acceptance of death, which must be dealt with unilaterally, on the other. It also closes the door on former ambitions and urgencies and very often shuts out other people, even the closest friendships. When impending death is closing the door on hope, the influence of a caring pastor can have profound significance in offering hope beyond death and courage for those waning days.

It is not an uncommon thing for a member of the family to suffer vicariously for the one who is dying and is already beyond the point of caring. Lois was very close to her father as he moved from hospital to home and to intensive care. He was kept under strong medication and part of the time was attached to life-sustaining apparatuses. Lois refused to accept his impending death, even though medical evidence seemed to point to nonrecovery, and she shut her mind to anything but completeness for her father. She kept herself away from friends and took on a new and completely different life-style. Even after his death she avoided any mention of him or any recognition of her father's passing. Resentments were the hinges on which her life seemed to swing while she went through days of deep depression. The minister could only stand by to take her hand at the moment she was ready to offer it.

It becomes difficult to separate the intertwining relationship of family and pastor, since both are affected directly in the interests of a common outreach. The patient, whose consciousness is consumed with the rejection of death and dying, is probably unaware of a deeper need found in the consolation from a caring pastor. And, to be sure, in the dying process the burden of initiative is endangered by the conditions of mobility on the part of the patient. The caring pastor finds the greatest opportunities and keenest responsibilities for ministry at this time. No moment of the past has called for greater empathy, patience, and understanding than when the pastor faces the perplexities of the patient, feels the throb of despair, and tries to understand this patient's anguish. The pastor attempts to come into this room of despair with strength and grace in order to support with assurance and faith. A relationship of personal identification can be established in this time of crisis that will produce assurance in the progression toward death. When life is blinded with tears, and death hangs stubbornly on the door latch, finite man encounters his point of greatest need. The pastor must speak his strongest exhortation here—not in apathy but in love and tenderness and with the force and authority of the Almighty.

When moving closer to the death scene, where the gradual release on life toward a firmer hold on death is taking place, the attitude of the patient becomes the focus of attention. Dr. Kubler-Ross has made significant studies on patients in their initial reaction to the facts of death and has followed them through the trauma until the moment of release. Her studies have brought her to a five-point list of stages through which she finds every patient traveling from the moment of awareness of impending death until that dreaded point of resignation to the inevitable.

The first stage is denial, when the patient refuses to accept the fact that death is imminent. This Kubler-Ross sees as being good, in that it acts as a cushion for the impact of such adverse news. This is followed by rage and anger over the fact that others will remain alive while he must die, using God as the target for the anger. Sensing the finality of the situation, the patient then begins a bargaining game with God in an effort to prolong life. A state of depression marks the fourth stage, when the patient is resigned to a state of personal grief and chooses to be left alone. The last stage is acceptance, when the patient knows that the end is very near and has complied with death in total resignation (1975, 10).

Even though Kubler-Ross is generally held in high regard for her studies in this area, Richard Schultz (1978, 71-76) does not give great credence to the five-point stage theory through which she takes the dying patient. He suggests that her work is "limited by its ambiguity, which is largely a product of the highly subjective manner in which her observations were obtained and interpreted." Schultz says that it appeared that she depended more on intuition to define a particular stage than on any systematic pattern of responses. And further, he questioned whether the patient actually goes through this sequence of stages or jumps from one to another. He also suggested that if the patients who were being interviewed were under drugged conditions, this would also have a significant bearing on the results obtained. He seems to rely more on other "attempts to plot the emotional trajectory of the dying patient with more objective methods against which to compare results."

Further studies by Hinton, Lieberman, and Weisman have been made and compared with Kubler-Ross, and these findings "cast doubt on the validity of a stage theory. Patients were not observed to go through stages, but rather to adopt a pattern of behavior that persisted until death."

Schultz finds a consensus among most writers on the subject of death that there are three major trends of terminally ill patients regardless of theories in stage of trend: the need to control pain; the need to retain dignity or feeling of self-worth; and the need for love and affection (76).

Whatever the pattern of behavior on the part of the patient in fulfilling the requirements imposed on him by death, it is incumbent upon the caring pastor to provide for him the best possible preparation in the final stages of living. Whether acceptance of death as a final stage of living is a natural phenomenon or a resignation controlled by a deep religious faith, it does bring into consideration the Christian hope for the patient. It is that hope that sees a full life after death and makes the acceptance and final resignation a beautiful acquiescence to an otherwise frightful experience. It is in this hope that Paul's observation takes on great meaning for the person in this crisis of life: "O death, where is thy sting? O grave, where is thy victory? . . . But thanks be to God, which giveth us the victory through our Lord Jesus Christ" (1 Cor. 15:55, 57).

Outside the realm of this hope, the patient faces death as a leap into a dark abyss with fear and trepidation. He knows there may be something out there, fearful or wonderful, but often there is no basis for making this judgment alone. Honesty and candor must be present in all pastor/patient relationships, and in no place is it more important than in dealing with life-and-death issues. In applying all the available wisdom and faith in the face of human inadequacies, valid communication and genuine relationships of trust must be established for this final moment of truth.

Whatever the function the pastor has performed in the past, or whatever the relationship is with the family at the present time, it is at this final stage of life where a very significant ministry can be effected. John Wynn looks at the relationship between the pastor and the families and states that "some pastors lack sufficient understanding of family life either to enjoy it themselves or to help parishioners with theirs. Sometimes they have been so busy in work for the Kingdom and so aloof from family living that they show less comprehension of family dynamics than do the laity" (1957, 182).

The decisive question is to what extent the minister is able to empathize with the family in the caring role. His commitment to love them cannot be expressed solely in the pulpit as he faces the grieving family for the Sunday worship. The gaping wound of suffering and despair is in evidence in the living room, the kitchen, and the den as well as in the sick-room. By dealing with the complete family relationship, the minister is able to provide real compassion and become an anchor for family stability. Here the patient/pastor relationship follows a pattern uncommon to other care providers who probably do not leave their office to be in the intimate family circle. After diagnosis and medical technology have led the patient to the end of their capacities and hope has flown away, it is the caring minister who must be waiting along the side of the road to bind up the broken spirit.

How small a portion of life we see and understand! Yet how much of the surface is exposed to the "fiery darts" of the enemy (Eph. 6:16). We have to stand back and let the sword fall where God means it to fall, for we cannot stand between Him and the object of His providence. But we need to know that God will never forsake the work of His own hands, and His "because" has covered the demands of our "why" at Calvary. We need to know that the big problems are not solved in the cloistered studies with a "Good morning, Lord" prayer.

How well I recall my first attempt at mending the rift of a broken marriage. On Saturday morning Charlie and Dottie came into my study in bitter accusation for the part the other partner was playing in their disintegrating relationship. I reached for my Bible and read Proverbs 5 to them about rejoicing with the wife of your youth (v. 18). Then I got them on their knees, placed my hands on their heads, and prayed long and loud while God was to begin His work of bringing it all together. Then I invited them to church on Sunday morning, pointed them to the door, and proceeded to thank God for helping me in salvaging the marriage.

But a strange thing happened! They did not come to church on Sunday morning. Their marriage broke up in a few weeks, and they never returned for further counseling. I was in ministerial shock!

I learned that the power of the enemy moves in where pastors tread, and our ministerial status exposes us openly to the most severe storms. Too often our greatest efforts and earnest desires turn most heavily against us. Sometimes even after prayer and fasting and giving our best, we will see a disintegration of those things for which we labored so hard.

But God has placed us in the role of ministers. Truth and goodness will stand the flames when our feet are treading in the ashes of our best efforts.

Bill and Mary had just shared with me the startling report of the doctor's examination made several days earlier. The diagnosis was cancer! Incurable! Mary passed me several promises she had quickly gleaned from her "Bread of Life" promise box in an attempt to elicit from God a commitment that Bill would not die. Each extracted promise had to do with riches from heaven. These left her in mental torment, for she thought God was accusing her of wanting her husband's insurance policy more than she wanted his health. Now she faced a deep sense of guilt mingled with the pain of separation that they both knew was imminent.

We carefully put aside the promise box, great as it might be in its proper place, and together we went through the various stages of dying until the final day of earthly separation arrived. Some days we did not even read the Bible. Some days we did not pray together. But each day brought us closer to the realization that God was working out His plan, in His own time, and doing it in ways beyond our understanding. This was especially true the day in the hospital when Bill won his roommate to the Lord and made a date with him, his first convert, to meet in heaven in a few short days. It was not a difficult task, the first Sunday morning after Bill's death and the day of the funeral, to preach to the family, "And we know that all things work together for good to them that love God, to them who are the called according to his purpose" (Rom. 8:28).

I had no idea how soon I would be testing the truth of the message I tried to preach to this broken family. It was in the cemetery that afternoon during Bill's funeral service that I suffered the previously mentioned heart attack and spent the following three weeks in the hospital.

One day during the next week a lady who had been in church that morning came to visit. Out of the cruelty of a troubled mind she sneered at me from the side of the bed, "Well, preacher, what do you think of Rom. 8:28 now? You try it on for size and see if you can wear it!" Then she left the room. She had hit a very sensitive spot, for the devil himself had beat her to it by several days. I had tried it on, and I did try to wear it, but it did not fit too comfortably. I was having trouble with it. I tried to make it over, to change the pattern and the style, but I did not do a very good job of it—nothing seemed to fit.

On my first Sunday back in the pulpit I preached again from Rom. 8:28. It was from a different perspective, to be sure, but how good it was to be able to tell my people that *"all* things work together for good to them that love God, to them who are the called according to his purpose" (italics added).

My visitor was there, and I sensed that she knew now that, by God's help, I was able to wear it!

There is a place for the Scriptures in dealing with death and the dying, but the purpose certainly goes much deeper than a mere traditional practice or an effort to follow a custom. The pastor must ask himself the questions, "What is the purpose of reading John 3:16, John 14, the Book of Revelation, or any other passage for that matter? What does the Bible passage say to this particular individual who at this moment is suffering the agonies of desolation? Is the imagery and message contained in this portion of the Word of God something with which this person can identify?"

The pastor must understand that the individual on the ministering couch does not hear the scripture as he hears it, nor is the patient coming from the study where time has been spent in meditation and prayer. The minister must be asking, "What will this mean to the patient?" But when the pastor, whose familiarity with the heartbeat of God has seasoned himself into a caring, loving, and understanding shepherd, takes the hand of the suffering one and quotes with tears in his heart, "Yea, though I walk through the valley of the shadow of death, I will fear no evil: for thou art with me . . . and I will dwell in the house of the Lord for ever" (Ps. 23:4, 6), God's peace will bring a settling influence to that troubled soul, and death, maybe for the first time, will have a different meaning.

The pastor's greatest purpose with the patient, as well as with the family, is to lay a foundation that will make death, and the grief to follow, as acceptable as possible. He is in essence asking, "How can I help you die?" and giving the assurance, "I will be there when you need me." For some people the refusal to grieve is as real as the denial of death.

Tom was a good member of my church, but he found it difficult to accept any biblical teaching on God's comfort in

40

times of grief. To him, tears were a sign of weakness, and sorrow showed a lack of faith in God. He was on hand to proclaim this conviction at every opportunity by relating personal experiences of how God had enabled him to overcome "without a tear." His contention was that any recognition of grief was damaging to one's Christian experience.

I think Tom really believed this, but it brought little comfort to the grieving person in the church and little help to the pastor who had to deal with the issue. The Bible tells us about "a time to weep, and . . . a time to mourn" (Eccles. 3:4). We are also encouraged to "rejoice with them that do rejoice, and weep with them that weep" (Rom. 12:15).

Probably at no time before the funeral will grief be so deep as when the family learns of an imminent death. The pastor should be on hand to support in any expression of these deep-seated emotions. The caring pastor is saying to them, "Let my heart be broken along with your heart, and let my tears mingle with your tears. Your grief is my grief, but let my hope be your hope!" He probably won't be able to bring back Lazarus from the dead, but when Bethany has been bereft of a loved one, he can weep with them in their sorrow.

4

The Pastor in Perplexity

There can be no more significant time in the work of the pastor than that moment when he moves out of his mundane routine and confronts a patient or family in their battle with death. This is the moment when all family structures are undergoing tremendous transformation while human relationships are threatened by the change. In this connection the minister stands with the family in the awareness of this important function. Even while he prays to be an instrument of stability in reshaping the meaning of life for them, he too is standing within the mysterious shadows of death.

The demands of the family are not as important an issue as the minister's apprehension about his own ability to cope with the death experience. Anxieties can be kept unnoticed in other areas of the ministry, but now there can be no artificial barriers erected for protection against human deficiencies. Here is where values and principles come under the most severe scrutiny. The standards of belief and support are on the line; they must be sincere, and they must be genuine.

When placed beside the patient as a helper in these days of distress and uncertainty, the minister's consciousness or self-recognition is important. This person has an acute awareness of the problem, as well as a keen sense of responsibility as a care provider, and is there in response to a need and remains there through a willingness to be involved in the patient's search for meaning and hope. The routine sources of security have vanished for the patient; therefore, support and strength must be found elsewhere. Often the minister becomes an almost complete provider of meaning in this difficult time. What does this mean? The situation may afford the rare privilege of introducing new values to hopeless people. This interpersonal relationship should not be decried but respected for the important place it holds in ministering to the one in need.

The minister also faces an awkward role as he enters into the highly technical medical environment. He often feels ill-prepared to handle the quandary. The sickroom, especially in hospitals, expresses itself in terms belonging to the medical profession. The patient usually comes under the pastor's influence for a few moments of visitation, while the rest of the time is spent under the impact of the medical environment with doctors, nurses, and hospital attendants. Even these few moments of pastor/patient interchange can be interrupted by routine hospital ministrations, leaving the minister as a bystander in the hallway. In this relationship the minister often feels threatened by the imposition while being given scant respect.

Kastenbaum and Aisenberg (1976, 184) outline some important phases in the role of the pastor and touch upon areas with which every minister can easily identify in the hospital room ministry: "Caught between the public role and private doubts, the minister may develop a defensive style of functioning." They further state that the consensus of clergy who have made a study of the role of other clergy in the death situation agrees that "one must function as a mature and sensitive person as well as a symbol of God and church," and that a "minister retains a significant role in the death system precisely because he does not have medical or technological functions to perform" (186).

43

In the act of ministering to the patient, the pastor is often frustrated. He does not wish to wield ecclesiastical power over the medical authorities but rather to seek harmony in the dichotomy of the professions. While making some off-duty rounds in a large city hospital with a doctor friend in an effort to harmonize some problems in this professional relationship with the patient, I asked his candid opinion on the role of the minister's work, as observed from his position. His comment was, "The minister could do so very much in support of the patient, but I see too many standing by the bedside, threatened and afraid, wondering, What do I do now? They could be a tremendous asset, both to the doctor and to the patient, especially when our battle is lost; but," he concluded, "too many times they are in the way."

I took issue with him at the time in defense of the clergy, but I had to admit to the truth of his observation, because I had been there too many times until hospital visitation had become a drudgery and an absolute nemesis. It was not because I did not want to minister but because I did not know how to work into the situation as a helper. How often I have wished my position could be more definitive as I viewed with envy the confidence with which the doctor seemed to be able to handle his part of the ministration with the suffering patient. As a result of my own lack of confidence and the lack of acceptance and understanding on the part of the medical profession, I have found the position to be a very lonely one.

While serving as a chaplain at a state institution, I was working with a fellow pastor in the geriatrics ward with a group of elderly women. My friend, a very serious chaplain, was expounding to them the deeper truths of the Scripture with great enthusiasm. It is difficult to know the value of some ministries until they are removed from us. We become so familiar with our routine that there is the danger of losing significance in the exercise. In this situation much of the ministry was lost in the enthusiasm of the moment rather than being captured by our congregation. One of the ladies, quite oblivious to the reality of the performance and not too impressed by the eloquence of the chaplain, looked at him and stated very flatly, "Boy, you've got to go! Yes, sir, you've got to go!" This response appeared amusing in this particular setting. But how often in an uncertain role, sensing that I was not being able to minister adequately to the patient, I have repeated these words to myself: "Boy, you've got to go! Yes, sir, you've got to go!"

On the other hand, there is the approach of the over-confident chaplain, as I witnessed recently in a gross misrepresentation of a loving and caring mission. The doctor had just shared his diagnosis of malignancy with the family, the cold facts of which had suddenly turned the light into darkness as hope had vanished into the night. Sitting in the family circle in the hospital room, I was trying to support the wife in her attempt to gain composure while the husband lay in bed sedated after his violent reaction to the news. At this point the hospital chaplain burst into the room, laden with clipboard and pamphlets, brushed past the family, and proceeded to shake the patient into a state of wakefulness. Endeavoring to identify his denominational affiliation, and spelling out the services that would be available to him in this crisis, the chaplain pressed for a positive response in a voice that could be heard several rooms away. In this exercise of duty, in the absence of pastoral concern, there was expressed in a routine performance a time-developed care without compassion. The family was completely ignored as a copy of the 23rd psalm was actually thrown on the bed, and, scribbling notes on a clipsheet, she left the room. The visit was concluded with another reminder of the services that could be rendered and their availability, if requested. The chaplain moved on to another room in her mission of mercy!

Rev. Robert Buxbaum (as cited by Kastenbaum and Aisenberg 1976) brings a unifying perspective to the place of the pastor and gives a valid reason for being. There can be no doubt in the crisis situation that the caring pastor has a unique task to perform, even though adequate standards may never be set up by which to judge performance. The following excerpt witnesses to the intimate relationship the caring minister can claim when standing by at the point of need.

> On the most significant level the [adequate] minister doesn't do anything in the sick room. He has not come to see the patient. He has not come to treat the patient. He has not come to perform any magical rites. He has come to be with the patient. Simply that. And yet, this is not very simple! The busy hospital routine is such that many people go in and out of the room during the patient's waking day. They come to feel, to feed, to provide, to take away, to treat, to inspect, to advise and on and on ad infinitum. It is the task of the pastor, and that which makes him so valuable a resource, *to be* with the patient (186).

All of this means a challenge for the great host of clergy who stand by, trusting that by being there a dimension of hope may be added for some encouragement and relief in the hour of sorrow and suffering. By being there, the minister is acting out faith and hope according to the needs that reveal themselves in a commitment of responsibility. In this attitude of honesty to self, as well as to the patient, is buried the shortcomings and fears as the minister seeks a place of freedom and respect.

When theology was referred to as the "queen of the sciences," the parson was paid in barter, along with the family doctor. The standards of conduct and behavior in each little community were set by the local minister, who took an active part in the care of the sick. The local parson stood by the bedside of the dying patient with the family doctor and rode in the horse-drawn hearse with the undertaker. They all shared in the trauma of sickness and death and received respect in accordance with the dignity of their individual office. This culture has changed drastically with the years until the fields of service have become dominated by economic competition and technical performances. The lines of communication have become static, and the channels of cooperation are clogged with professionalism.

The doctor has to be a specialist in a particular field of research with a reputation for excellence before effectively attending to our physical needs. Compensation is meted out in proportion to the degree of medical expertise. The undertaker has become a sophisticated mortician, attended by an entourage of sleek sedans, plush hearse, and flower cars so that our bodies can be carried to their final resting places with the honor that society has demanded. The material value placed upon this service is still the subject of much controversy and question. The minister, threatened by professionalism, medical science, and the sleek caravan, takes a stance at the bedside, knows what is expected of him, and acts without thought of reward or compensation. In this entire spectrum of service all that is sought is a partnership with respect and dignity in the arena staged for the healing and helping ministry. In cooperation with peers and in the final definition of service the minister hopes to be able to open the door to hope and confidence in the dying moments of the patient.

Dr. Kubler-Ross, seeing the many functions necessary for the well-being of the patient in the work of the minister, speaks about the "transprofessional domain" (1975, 12). This puts the patient in the center of activity, where all the areas of service should be available and everybody dealing with the sick person would develop their skills to the full. Then she comments on the clergy in the following words:

In the hospital the clergy have only recently re-gained some meaning, some entry, and some role. The clergy deserve a significant place not only in helping the dying patient, but in serving as a resource to the patient's family and, hopefully, to the physician or to other health professionals who are troubled by the burden placed upon their shoulders *(ibid.).*

So, in the context of the "transprofessional domain," the minister becomes part of a team effort that eliminates the position of helplessness and offers the recognition deserved by professionals. But Kubler-Ross also senses the awkward position in the intermingling of medical personnel blurring the lines of activity instead of finding a clarification of duties. She points out that "the clergy are, in all faiths, the spokes-men or representatives of a higher power. As they seek to hope and to offer support, it is within the context of personal imperfection and lack of complete authority. By contrast, medicine has been given by our society the aura of having the final authority in dealing with health, illness and death" (1975).

The relationship between medical staff and the clergy could easily be one of compatibility rather than competition. I have discovered that self-complacency on the part of either profession can result in the alienation of an otherwise unique partnership of participation in the welfare of the patient. However, I have never met with rebuff when the overture for a share in the interest of the patient was initiated in a profes-sional manner. A danger on the part of either participant is failure to appreciate all the implications of immediacy in need and service as related to the other person's particular profession. Here is where traditions, authority, standards, and structures can become barriers to the cooperative healing process. The pendulum swings from tolerance to intolerance and from compatibility to competition, and all of the proba-bilities for a caring ministry are commandeered in its sway of influence.

The doctor has come and made a pronouncement of death in the recognition of medical limitations and has left the scene. A deep depression with a cloud of darkness has settled in upon the home. The family is left with the stunning verdict that death is going to visit them. There is no logic behind all of this, and little fair play can be justified at the moment. Often the family is unable to understand any involvement of a greater power in responsibility or concern. The fact of death settles upon them, and their minds are closed to any solution of problems resident within the pronouncement, other than the fact that they have to accept the consequences.

It is here that the pastor takes a stand and attempts to lead the family into accepting the reality of the moment, offering faith and strength in the critical days of adjustment. If it has been discovered that the family has been nurtured in the Christian faith, the pastor will be able to offer a future hope for the loved one who has been stricken with illness. Often clergy find themselves meeting families where the first encounter with death is in the context of the present crisis. Persons who live in the involvement of a religious faith can grasp the significance of a transition from one life to another as they are thrust into a death situation. This acknowledgment can give hope to a distraught family in anticipation of a continued relationship with the loved one.

The minister should always be looking out for larger opportunities of service and be preparing for any exercise of faith and usefulness that would minister to the sufferer. It is not an uncommon thing for the pastor to be confronted with a request for divine healing. The pastor must respond to this tremendous possibility of healing through faith by way of prayer, anointing, and the laying on of hands (James 5:14-15). He should not be so concerned with preparing the family for death that he overlooks the possibilities of healing.

There is danger in expending our interest in that which is external without combining the inward with the outward and taking a deep interest in all that pertains to the Christian ministry. It is not uncommon to meet a modern Paul who cries out, "Lord, take away the thorn," but, unlike the apostle, responds in anger when he hears the answer, "My grace is sufficient for thee" (2 Cor. 12:7-9).

George was dying from diabetes. He had endured extensive surgery and was in danger of further complications. He had been to several places of healing without the desired results. Having known him as a hard-drinking, hard-living, and hard-driving man, I was unprepared to meet such a religious person on my vacation to my hometown. When he asked me to place my hand on him and heal him, my faith took leave of absence.

After talking to him about spiritual healing, I soon discovered his absolute lack of interest. Then I said quite candidly, "George, I am not going to heal you, because all you want your strength for is so that you can have one more rip-roarin' drunk before you die and go to hell!" He answered me in equal candor and told me where I could go and to take all the rest of the clergy with me. In my closing prayer with him we were both using the same language but poles apart in their application. George wanted healing on his own terms apart from the grace of God to sustain if the healing were not forthcoming.

God does heal! But many times sickness and suffering remain, and often bitterness and discouragement remain with it. Here the pastor can help the patient through the trauma, not in the desperation of resignation, but in faith and renewed hope. Dimension can also be added in the dilemma by helping the patient see that he can view the whole ministry of redemption where there is no place for condemnation. When the patient is moved by fear and overcome by anxiety, the man of God can show the suffering one that it is meant to serve a higher spiritual purpose.

In the family where faith has not been formulated into a living relationship with God, this could become a point of stability for the brokenhearted loved ones. The pain of the realization of loss will not be minimized, but in the crisis of dilemma they will be able to accept it by faith. "The Christian doctrines of death and the resurrection provide a very valuable [resource] tool for understanding" (Irion 1954, 76).

The message of the comforting Gospels is that there are no accidents in God's economy. We can look upon everything in life as an event with a divine and beneficent purpose underlying the whole of it. To be sure, this will lead to inquiry and to the place of prayer, but it will also lead to a deeper trust and the expectation of meeting God at every turn. The pastor must know this, for he will sooner or later face the violence of the opposing forces of life. For the mystery of death brings down the crushing blow as the minister stands with the distraught parents before the little white coffin to hear the haunting question, "Preacher, tell me why . . . !"

I was only a teenager when Betty died; but one day, as a minister, I visited the home still suffering from the loss, while the father in anger and accusation asked, "Preacher, why did my baby have to die such a horrible death—and only two years old?" And I listened while a brokenhearted father poured out curses on the cruelty and unfairness of God.

No amount of theological exercise on original sin or philosophizing on the problem of guilt will satisfy the inquiry. No matter how eloquently spoken, the words "The Lord gave, and the Lord hath taken away; blessed be the name of the Lord" (Job 1:21) can be smothered in sobs of grief and curses of deprecation. When you have finished, there still remains the loss with its question. And the "why" is not asked of the medical profession, but it is handed to the minister to handle, and an adequate "because" is expected.

51

The grief-stricken face the suffering and pain of the moment, while the pastor tries to reach for the ultimate meaning in the wisdom and the eternal order of God. Is there any way to unite the extremes of the dilemma or to pull together the polarization so apparent in the problem?

Paul Tillich, preaching from Isaiah 40, speaks about "moving continually between the depths of human nothingness and the great heights of divine creativity," and suggests that we belong to "both of them every moment of our life and history" (1948). Maybe the answer is hidden in this insight into life as it relates to grief. Out of "the depths of human nothingness" (man's greatest fear, anxiety, and grief) comes the great reconcilement of all contradictions as we rise to the "heights of divine creativity" (man's greatest hope—love).

This love must go further than our intellect, or it is not the love portrayed by God through His Son, Jesus Christ. For in the final analysis love is not a theory, nor is a parent's aching heart for a dying child an illusion. You must feel the pain with the parents. You must know it in your heart as part of a divine operation. You must have an understanding that cannot be put into words. For what was looked upon as death was in reality the gift of eternal life. Instead of victory for the enemy, it was defeat for the forces of darkness. And only in this hope can there be found a power greater than the grief.

How can I make the cursing, brokenhearted father see that in the providence of God these destructive forces do not overcome love? How can I make him understand that the bonds that bind one to God's fulfilling love cannot be broken by death? How can I make him understand that "in all these things we are more than conquerors through him that loved us" and that "neither death, nor life . . . shall be able to separate us from the love of God, which is in Christ Jesus our Lord" (Rom. 8:37-39).

The preacher himself may be able to understand the simplicity of the answer, but a special relationship with God is necessary for that brokenhearted father to find comfort in the message.

One of the most difficult problems in facing an untimely death for the individual, as well as for the family, is the problem of thwarting God's purpose for that individual to "grow in fulfillment and integration, overcoming the personal affliction and problems of life" (Irion 1954, 76) and to be able to live out that threescore and 10 years upon this earth in happiness and worthwhileness. The values and purposes of life are suddenly broken loose while the family searches for a reason. A Christian faith and commitment can offer the family and the individual a chance to rebuild, to rethink, and to relive a new set of purposes and values, thereby helping to free the painful reality resident in the recent loss. "Securing release from the pain of loss is not an act of disrespect to our loved ones. It frees us from a more wholesome reverence. We are then ready to face and to understand the implications of belief in immortality" (Rogers 1950, 30). Being able to lead the family along this darkened pathway into the light of realization, the pastor becomes a source of strength and stability. This servant brings the family a positive faith in their search and development in the struggle for understanding and freedom.

When the doctor has made the pronouncement "It's only a matter of time" and has concluded that the only help the medical profession can give is in relieving the physical suffering to the end, the burden falls to other resources in the provision of care and strength in the anticipation of death. It has been observed that our cultural pattern reinforces the fear of death. Since medical science is making it possible for life to be prolonged, the pastor is in a dilemma. He is squeezed between a fear on the one hand from which death would be a release and the faint glimmer of hope that God may still impart His healing grace.

Does the pastor attempt to placate the fear while taking the liberty of aborting the possible hope, or does he try to fan the spark of hope while attempting to relieve anxiety when the imminence of death appears certain? Does the pastor enter the sickroom, overcome by a sense of finality, face the reality of death with the family, and assume the freedom of decision in preparation for the final moments of life? Only a pastor with a mature and loving relationship with the family could share the responsibility of such value judgment and act accordingly.

Bill suffered a stroke several years ago and never fully recovered. One day he slipped into a comatose state and was taken to the hospital, where he lived for two months on life-sustaining equipment. The diagnosis was not encouraging, and he was becoming more and more dependent on the machine as a life support. The weight of responsibility grew heavier as the family reached out for support and a voice of decision. The pastor, standing where extremes meet, could find no basis for hope, yet could not feel that the vital decision belonged to him.

He stood by in support as the family fanned the spark of hope, combined with a flame of faith, and treated the father and husband as a complete person. Sustained by a deep religious faith that was to be tested, as well as the love and support from a caring pastor, they waited in hope. Bill did return home and was able to walk, talk, laugh, and greet his friends; and he carried on with considerable alacrity for several months before his death.

This brings up issues too great to pursue here. I am not sure that religious faith needs to judge or stand in judgment, nor is the heavy burden to be placed upon the pastor for making the decision when human help has reached its limitations, in a situation for which there is little precedent for counsel. But when the decision has been made, the pastor can add strength in respecting the deep feelings involved when other resources are utterly exhausted. It must be understood that the family cannot know what course will work out for the best in a society that in some ways cares so much and yet in other ways cares so little for human life.

William W. Zeller states that even though values are everybody's business, they are, nonetheless, considered to be in the province of philosophers and clergy. He further states: "During illness the patient is confused about his own personal value system because of his internal emotional conflicts and because he is under unusual stress. Not unfrequently he comes into treatment with fears, doubts, misgivings and a lack of basic trust." As the successful outcome of the hospital procedures depends in a large measure on the doctor/patient relationship, so too must there be a solid pastor/patient relationship and trust in the exchange of values.

Assuming that the patient is terminally ill or kept under abnormal conditions in which he is not able to function, it may be possible to lead him through his fears in a pastor/patient relationship until they can be reassessed into a set of personal values. This, in essence, is a reinterpretation of reality and can also be an integral part of the patient's well-being.

Dr. Peter Giovacchine writes about suicide among the adolescent and makes an observation that could well apply to the patient whose encounter with death is as real as it is to the suicidal adolescent. He states that they "need to draw upon our strength, our patience, our resilience, and our compassion. Our relationship with them . . . is the best means to test and re-evaluate our values and our way of life" (1981, 189-90). Leading the patient through this trauma could result in a new concept of faith, or it could be a reaffirmation of faith for the one standing on the threshold between life and death.

Even though there is no justification for passing moral judgment on the suffering person, it nevertheless behooves the pastor to be able to "give . . . a reason [for] hope" (1 Pet. 3:15) when the personal value system of the patient breaks down in the sickroom. Here the clergy can fulfill the greatest function and lead the patient through the valley of fear into the light of hope and assurance of faith in these final days of illness when all other avenues of hope have been closed to the suffering one.

The whole movement of pastoral support reaches the ultimate when you sit with a family in the crowded courtroom, awaiting judgment equal in terror only to the diagnosis of terminal illness by the medical profession. The black-robed judge enters the chambers to pronounce the awful sentence, broken by sobs of emotion, ". . . you have been found guilty as charged, and shall pay for your crime with your life. On [and he gives the date], I sentence you to be hanged by the neck until you are dead, and may God have mercy on your soul."

Amid the shock of disbelief and stunned emotions the dreadful truth that "the society that protects life also has the power to take it" settles on the courtroom. The pastor is caught in the middle of two factions equally needing support. The accusers are there, but now they discover little satisfaction in the sentence they so ardently sought. The parents of the defendant return home to face the consequences of this satisfaction of justice. Worse still, they go out to face a society determined to remind them that they are the parents of a murderer. These things are not forgotten like a dream but live on as a nightmare, haunting, accusing, defying, and hating.

Thankfully I did not have to stand with the families through the agonizing days and final moments when the black flag would be raised and lowered telling us that justice had been carried out. The sentence was later commuted to life imprisonment. But I learned that while both sides stand apart in rebellion, and both sides are asking different questions, they are confronted with the same evil whose mystery has darkened their night. But it was the same message to both sides that showed them that there was something better than vengeance. We learned together that the message that condemns is also the message that heals, for the same God who said, "Thou shalt not kill," also is the One who says, "I forgive." And I saw that only the quiet pressure of the truth of God's love could effect a reconciliation, bind severed relationships, and heal the wounded hearts. And I learned that only as we are able to stand by in care and concern, albeit in despair and fear, and reach out in our desolateness to the Omnipotence of heaven can there be any hope for healing in that mystery that only the heart can understand.

Throughout the entire caring ministry the pastor is found to be encompassed in an environment of conformity to various routines, measured by a desire to help, with the welfare of the patient as the primary intent. The pastor discovers that courage, strength, understanding, and love are the ingredients of his personal contribution, and these are dispensed without prescription to the one in need. I have walked this route from Jerusalem down to Jericho and back again, for nearly 40 years; but it was not until after many years on the journey that I felt any justification for laying claim to the Samaritan role of binding up the broken spirit. The role was not discovered in an attempt to infringe on the jurisdiction of other staff or professional ministrations. However, I have carried out services in the delivery room, the operating room, the recovery room, the ward, and the kitchen for which neither Scripture reading, prayer, nor seminary training could give adequate preparation. In an effort to place my strength in the middle of a very interdependent structure, without compromise or apology, I discovered acceptance proportionate to my willingness and ability to become involved. I came to the task as a care provider, with a message whose beginning and ending was love, and the hands in pain reached out for support.

Mary was a patient in the intensive care unit, where hope had faded for her recovery from a serious operation. The doctors had performed their tasks and had left the scene: "We have done all that we can do." The door was opened to the waiting minister. As the staff carried on in the performance of their tasks about the unit, I attempted to bring healing to a soul with the assurance of God's love, while her body weakened and suffered pain. In those brief moments by her bedside we held hands together. We cried together. We prayed together and repeated some familiar verses of Scripture. She asked many questions, and I confess that I was able to answer only a few of them. But I sensed that those answers were not of prime consequence because we had anchored our faith in an all-wise God who knew, cared, and was in control in the face of death as well as life.

The violence of the system was very much in evidence, and I sensed others' resentment for my intrusion as I prayed aloud by the bedside. Nor did it immediately decrease in intensity as I invited the staff in a small circle around the foot of the bed, where I prayed for them. I prayed for a healing touch of love in the important part of their ministry to the sick and dying. I prayed for each of them individually, as well as for their families, whom I had never met. I prayed for their health and asked God for strength for them in the burdensomeness of their professional tasks. Then I prayed that each one of them might find a large place in their hearts for God, in whatever context of His revelation would meet their need.

All the barriers of this compact community of workers

collapsed into a unity of spirit as we stood in a very small circle, holding hands. I do not suppose that a report of this particular ministry was ever recorded in the hospital records that night, but neither was I ejected from the intensive care unit. Nor was there resentment when I hugged that nurse and put my arms around a gruff technician. When I looked into the tear-filled eyes of the young intern and said, "God bless you, son," there was no anger. As I walked out of the room, I heard someone say, "Thank you, Reverend, thank you!" I sensed that a tiny opening had been made in a doorway to a very special ministry.

I had now entered into an arena that belonged to the minister. It was that area where fear is swallowed up in faith, and the liberating power of God makes the spirit free. It was the area of the soul of one woman whose body was nearing the end of its usefulness, facing the moment when spirit reaches out to spirit and faith bridges the gap. In the brief moment that was shared with one dying woman and with God, love was also extended into the continuum of the living. My firm belief is that through the framework of faith in a God of love and understanding, combined with courage to stand in the crisis, the most effective relationship between pastor and family can be discovered.

Conclusion

In conclusion, let us review the fabric of a pastor/patient relationship. What constitutes help in the mind and capabilities of every other supporter in the sickroom is different from that of the pastor. Clergy serve in a very unique capacity as they minister to a need that is often concealed in the insatiable quest for living. Much pastoral expertise is carried out in an informal setting when pastor and patient meet at the point of life's greatest need—meaning at the moment of death. How often one finds that the greatest service is rendered simply by being with the patient. The pastor does not enter the scene as a theologian, philosopher, technician, or even as a solver of problems; the pastor's role is to help the grief-stricken and to walk with them through the valley of sorrow, listening for the hidden cries for help, bridging the chasm between despair and hope, and offering a helping hand for the passage. When the trauma of suffering and death engulf and threaten, the pastor is there with hope and assurance to sustain through the diminishing relationships with reality. In the final analysis, the pastor is there to help the patient face the immediate situation by demonstrating a firm faith in God who loves to the end and to give assurance that He is standing by.

But the last word must be said for the patient, who holds the all-important position of translating personal pain into purpose and preparation. To this one we say: Find comfort from Him who, when He was reviled, answered not in kind, and when He was beaten and belittled, opened not His mouth in defense. But when He battled the enemy forces that included death, He cried out, "Let this cup pass from me!" (Matt. 26:39); and on the Cross He asked, "Why . . . ?" (27:46; Mark 15:34). And the answer echoed back from eternity, "Because . . . of love!" So, when your tears of agony and despair flow, understand that love transcends human suffering and that there is hope and redemption in the eternal plan of God.

Epilogue

To dress up these words would thwart their purpose. Some were written in the subway, some in the hospital waiting room. Some were scribbled from the side of the bed sometime in the night, while some were written from a park bench in Boston Common. All were written on the run, alone and afraid! They were taken from the daily diary of a pastor on a journey through the death scene—his own! They are too personal to share, except that in the spirit of sharing another might find hope.

Friday, May 25

Word from the biopsy came through. Negative! "You seem to be in good health. Come back in six months for your usual checkup."

Monday, May 28

The middle of the morning the phone rang. I answered it. "You are to report to New England Medical Center to Dr. H. on Wednesday at 11. I have talked to Arthur, and he has arranged for—"

"Why?"

"In further study of your tests we have discovered cancer cells. We need to take immediate action."

"No! It can't be possible that I have cancer. You said—"
"Further studies have revealed . . ."
CANCER!

I sat down and tried to run this through my mind. Over and over. Again and again. Is this real? Am I having a dream?

My whole world fell apart as I watched an entire lifetime unfold before me in a few minutes. The utter worthlessness of so much that had value just a few minutes before was now laughing in my face as I suddenly began to sift out the real. The yesterdays tumbled into today, and life became a jumbled jigsaw puzzle; and I was searching through the heap for an identifiable piece to begin construction. My life began to recede as God's eternity began to plug the gap.

Called President Nease and asked for a few minutes of his time. I told myself I would be brave and cool and must not break down in front of him. I had to run this by someone—I needed a friend. How dependent we really become in the crisis!

He came out from behind his desk and sat down to listen. He said, "Ken, take your time; my day (and night, too, if necessary) is yours." I fell apart. He listened. I bawled and blubbered and walked around the office, until I finally got it out of my system. He placed his arm around me and prayed, and for the moment the whole problem seemed to fade into the great mystery of God's overpowering love.

I went out to try to face the inevitable in faith and not in fear. God's eternity—my life! Somewhere in there, there must be meaning! How to find it.

The week was filled with visits to the doctors and meetings with the social worker and various personnel and units about the hospital. Warnings on possible ill effects. Considered other options. Pamphlets to read, and decisions to make. Decided on radium treatments. Off to the measuring room and the indelible pencil marks.

Felt like I was being prepared and given the last meal, getting ready for the final walk in the morning to the chair or to the rope. Other people were sitting around the room waiting. One man had an **X** marked on the side of his head, while others had various identifying spots in critical places. In spite of evidences of anxiety in the room human nature came through with its bits of humor as one old gent asked if they were marking him up for jumper cables.

I watched for the marks on my body. We were being reduced to signs. Or just numbers. Will the outside world forget us?

A bunch of miserable comforters suffering in our own vanity and speaking complicated words to people who tried not to understand.

Tuesday, June 5

Beautifully tattooed. X rays and radium treatment. Nothing strange seems to be happening except a bit of nausea.

Wednesday, June 6

Treatment and routine work.

Thursday, June 7

Treatment. Nausea. No appetite. Met with dietitian. List of foods I should be taking. Not much appetite. Food repulsive. Morning sickness—wonder if this is a medical first?

Friday, June 8

Radium treatment at 12. Boston—I must eat some food along the way to keep my stomach from deteriorating. That's what the man said, anyway.

Scan at Carney at 1:45—no food or drink before then. Between a rock and a hard place. You'll die if you don't eat, and it will kill you if you do. Never did want to die on an empty stomach, but who cares!

I took the subway back to Ashmont and walked to Carney. The sun was very hot, and I was overcome by dizziness. I met a kind man who suggested I go to the park and sleep it off. Drink a quart of liquid on top of a very queasy stomach. IV and injection. How can you keep your dignity with a puke pan in your hands? Finally over. Walked back to subway and home.

Sick enough to die and wish I could. But I don't.

Saturday and Sunday

Blessed relief from "The Machine."

Monday, June 18

Here we go again after week of routine treatment. If that is routine, what on earth will the real thing be like? Have always said that I'd never go through this; but when the chips are down and you are grasping for straws, I guess it looks a bit different.

I go to the Purple Room (all the "prison" robes are purple) and change into my johnny. Now I go to the waiting room, where I enter another world of people who are also waiting.

I am a cancer patient, and I join a group of other cancer patients. You lose all identification unless you have an **X** mark on your head or on your chest, or some other visible part. At this stage there are more visible parts than your dignity would have allowed. But it doesn't seem to make any difference now.

Then the thing that I hoped would not happen, happened! The voice over the intercom announcing the next victim blared, "Reverend Sullivan, you're next!" "Reverend" —you become a symbol. Eyes turn in your direction, and ears are opened. One comedian sneers, "Do preachers get cancers too? I thought they healed people." And I cringed and hurt on the inside.

Vacant stares assume an air of hope; hungry eyes turn to you as if the Lord himself had entered their world, and they reach for His garment. Barriers break down while stories and problems run free. They reach out for hope and cheer. Inside I am crying, "How can I help you? Don't you see that I am one of you? I have cancer, too! Why do you think I am here?" But they can't hear, and they keep reaching out.

I come out of the room, dizzy and nauseated, while Mrs. T. pleads, "Reverend, why don't you pray for us." Mrs. G. responds, "It's too late, Father, most of us are already over the hill." But a camaraderie develops around a common bond, and we share our anxieties and pain. They reach out to me, but ironically I am one of them. The best that I can do is listen.

Mrs. C. has no family and few friends, and her home is in another country. I asked God why He couldn't have spared her suffering and grief. Hers transcends all others, for she cries alone and is afraid. Maybe the reason Jesus had such a great following while He was here on earth was because people knew He would listen with a broken heart when they told Him about their deep hurts.

Big men, young women, grandmothers, and dignified business people sit together waiting for "The Treatment." Some joke about the "Electric Chair." Some are bitter and angry and curse and talk about their worldly possessions—now gone! Some are frightened, for they are sure the end is very near. Some hold on in hope for many days yet ahead after "The Treatment." Some try to be cool and casual, covering a deep fear of the inevitable. Some are sure they are going to beat "this thing."

But we are all there, waiting, hoping; waiting, hoping; waiting, hoping; while something moves us to struggle on through "The Machine" and its consequences. It is tough to cry alone, and in a very real sense the hurt cannot be shared.

Tuesday, June 19

Back to Boston and "The Treatment." Very sick. Outside Boylston Station I had to sit on the park bench before I had the strength to proceed further. The abdominal pain is now almost more than I can bear.

Don picked me up at the station and took me out to dinner. He told me he had been praying for me. I appreciated it but had no appetite. He, too, is a hurting man. I listened while he recounted the details of his wife's longtime illness and recent death. He needed to talk about it, and I tried hard to listen. It's a hurting world, and I must not make my problems so big that no one can get over these barriers to my heart.

But, God, why did I want to scream out at him, "Don't you know that I am sick and that I am going to die, and it hurts me to listen to you? Let me tell you my problems." Thank You, God, for helping me to keep it all on the inside just between us.

Oh, the pain! I can't take much more. Pete called tonight and simply said, "I'm praying for you." I felt better.

Thursday, June 21

I met with the doctor today and felt pretty good. Pain seems to be easing off—or am I becoming immune to suffering? Can one die with cancer and not hurt?

I felt sorry for the doctor. He tried so hard to be professional and keep it all to himself. How much does he know that he doesn't want to tell me? Inside I wanted to holler as loud as I could, "Yes, I know I have cancer and am going to die, and we both know it. Why don't we sit down and talk about it together?" Tell me.

But I have been in his position so many times—your heart hurts, but your speech is dumb. My heart went out to him, and I took him by the arm and said, "It's OK, Doc, we're going to beat this thing; by God's help we are going to beat this thing." I don't know if it made him feel any better, but he said, "Well, I hope so," and he left the room.

He came back again and said, "You know, you have four more weeks to go." Oh, no! I'll never make it!

Monday, June 25

I guess it's possible to fix your mind on one thing so much that you miss the meaning and purpose of everything else. But, God, I didn't ask for cancer, and I don't know what You are trying to do to me. The exposed places are getting raw, and the doc told me today that I might need surgery. Is there no end?

Tuesday, June 26

Blood today! Oh, I hate that ever-piercing needle. How can I take any more of this? I'm sick. Karl called and wants to take me to Boston tomorrow. It is difficult to accept this, but coming from a good friend I know he means what he says. I hate to be beholden to people or have them wait on me. I've always been independent and could get by on my own. I wonder if this is a forerunner of what the days ahead are going to be like. Well, I guess people do need people, but how to accept giving from others. I am very awkward over some things—this is one of them. It is much easier to give. You can do that and forget about it. I do appreciate his offer.

Wednesday, June 27

Met an old friend today who asked, "Ken, are you in pain or something? Your eyes don't look good, and you are acting like you are in pain." I wanted to say, "Oh, didn't you hear that I have cancer, and right now my guts are on fire, and I'm slowly dying, slowly dying, slowly dying!" But I knew if I told him I would have to listen to all the sordid details of the death of all his relatives who died with a bigger cancer or who were about to die. And I was not prepared to share the martyr role of all his misfortunes. I made a joke of it and told him that I was drinking too much coffee, and it kept me awake at night.

Does anyone really care that I have cancer? Can I sit down with someone and share the real ugly truth about what's happening? Does anybody care that I walk the floor at night doubled up in pain or stagger across Boston Common on my way to "The Machine"? Does anyone care that I have to hang on to the rail in the Proger Building until I can get strength enough to walk to the subway and get home? Does anyone care that I am going to die?

Thursday, June 28

Doc gave me some medication for stomach problems. Thinks I should see the social worker for "ventilation," whatever that means. Maybe he thinks I am going daft and need to have further attention. I don't think I need it, but I guess maybe I have been acting a bit odd.

Anyway, it will be good to see how the professionals deal with an old ornery patient-in-dilemma. Interesting how it looks from this side of the table when the pros are confronted with the "why me?" inquiry. Hope I can pick up some good pointers.

I had always assumed that cancer and insanity were for other people and that they were supposed to accept it as a routine part of living. Have discovered that they are as devastated as I am. Well, maybe if I do live, I will be a better counselor.

Friday, June 29

I am not a very patient patient. I kick like a steer in a stall for the first time. And I don't seem to be too much help to those dear people in the group with me. They look to me for help, and sometimes I am bitter and wish they would leave me alone. My pain is as bad as theirs. Sometimes I ask God to forgive me, and then I am able to encourage them a bit. Often we cry together and share, and it seems to help a bit; but I seem to be missing something here—I can't get a handle on it, and I often complain.

Monday, July 2

Had a very rough time this weekend. Nothing seemed to go right. Discouraged and afraid.

Something strange happened this afternoon! The pain in my lower parts suddenly eased off, and I felt good all over. It came like a cleansing. Like a big hand washed me clean from the top of my head to the soles of my feet. Could it be the healing hand of God? He is able to do this—He has done it before. Paul said to me at the beginning of this ordeal, "What will people say someday when you are healed of this thing?" Do I dare to claim it, or shall I wait and see? I do not know what is happening, but my pain is gone.

Just called Pete and told him that I felt better, and he said, "I know," and proceeded to tell me when it happened. He said, "I prayed for you today, and for a moment I lost touch with the world. God gave me the assurance . . ."

Tuesday, July 3

Appointment with the doctor after the treatment. He examined the danger areas and said he could not find any evidence: "It seems to be cleared up, and I am pleased with what I have found." Thank the Lord, it is going to be OK. I shared the whole process with Paul. He understood. He, too, had prayed.

The fellowship of sufferers is thickening—we look to each other for support. I never dreamed that I would be part of a select group of cancer victims. Lord, help me to be able to share with them something of Your healing power! Maybe yet He can work out something beautiful from this experience.

Thursday, July 5

Regular treatment. Time with the doctor, nurse, social worker, and another doctor. They did quite an extensive examination. No hurts, no pain, and the problem seems to have gone. They can't understand "apart from a miracle" why I feel so well. Talked to Paul again tonight, and his conclusion was, "God is working."

One man left our group today, and as he left he said, "Let's keep praying for each other."

Friday, July 6

"And Can It Be!" Paul played it so beautifully last Sunday night on his cello. No pain. No hurt.

Monday, July 9

Much X rays with new marks and needles to reduce the field of concentration. "We are putting you on a couple of weeks of new treatment."

Tuesday, July 10

Final treatment on the "Big Machine." Wonder what the minor "concentration" is going to be like? I might as well die on a big machine as a small one.

On the way home by subway I met an interesting man. He was either under strong intoxication or had been dealt an uneven game hand. He kept up a constant chatter and addressed his comments to the best listener. He kept repeating, "Did you ever sit down to figure it all out?" I wanted to say to him, "Yes, I have, but I am not sure I have found the answer. If you know it, tell it to us."

He followed up with, "I've always believed, and my father always told me, 'It's nice to be nice.'" Disappointed! Thought we were going to get some great bit of hitherto unrevealed philosophy. Well, maybe he's not too far off the track!

A bit of philosophy that probably few fellow riders have ever accepted. There are some things that are beyond trying to figure out. But somewhere in the secret chambers of eternity I suppose there is an answer. Why are we so gung ho about answers—are there not some things that defy an understandable answer?

Did God really heal me from this cancer? Why am I still taking treatments? Why did I feel sicker today than I did yesterday?

I do not know why I have cancer, and in the final analysis I don't suppose the "why" is so vital. There are so many things that go beyond and are much deeper. Aren't the basics the same anyway?

It is "nice to be nice." And if out of this I can make the way easier for another person coming down the trail, or treat the fellow sufferer with more compassion, love, and understanding, it doesn't matter too much, I suppose, if I can't figure it out. I will try to be "nice."

Wednesday, July 11

New machine, new surroundings, and new people. Different treatment that doesn't seem so difficult. But the same terror and fear and grasping! Again I hear it, and again I am not prepared for the burden—"Oh, we have a reverend with us, and he has cancer too." Didn't You know, God, that preachers are not supposed to get cancer? Why am I here? Did You make a mistake somewhere? If You did heal me, why didn't I have faith enough to quit "The Machine" and leave? But the doctor said, "We want to try this." And I groan, and I am afraid. I want to reach out and help and touch these others with a healing touch. But I can't, and it mocks me, for I have cancer, too!

But didn't God heal you? Why are you here? The questions pile up, and the doubts pile up, and this "reverend," who is supposed to have all the answers, and to know all there is to be known about the ills and hurts of humanity, is down there where the doubts and questions are. And he crawls and flounders with the rest of them, and he does not dare to let them know. Where are You, God?

O God, through it all, help my faith, and help me to be "nice," and maybe I can reach someone who is reaching out for a friend.

Thursday, July 12

Counseled with Joe tonight at church. His problems were so big I forgot to groan about mine. I believe I was able to hear him better tonight than the last time we met. We talked together. We prayed together. We cried. I seem to cry much easier these days. Am I getting soft? I am trying to be nice. Or am I going off my rocker?

Friday, July 13

Routine! "You are supposed to meet with your doctor today." What is one supposed to do with his Irish superstition, when on Friday the 13th he is suddenly summoned into the doctor's office?

It was a new substitute—a student intern who was using me as his guinea pig. Not too impressed by his learning experience. Tried to give him some lessons on patient handling and care. But I did not impress him with my expertise.

Informed that I was having 12 more treatments. Wow! I thought I was cured and that the report would be that I was through. New pains are cropping up again—maybe the cancer is coming back! I am hurting, I am afraid, and I am discouraged.

"We have a preacher here, and he has cancer too" keeps mocking me. Groan.

Problem came up today about camp with the grandkids. They need the camp, so I guess I have to find some courage somewhere and take on the responsibility for a couple of weeks down the road. I can do it—I think!

Glen called and asked a lot of questions, but I could not give him many answers. Guess they still are interested in "old pop."

One man in a serious state of cancer philosophized today (in trying to keep up his courage). We have to take it "one day at a time—accept each day as it comes." I suppose he had seen that on a bumper sticker.

I have been trying to run this through the mill, and I am not sure that it comes out right. The quality of today can be greatly influenced by yesterday. And tomorrow's quality will be the result of today's preparation. So if yesterday was a preparation for today, I do have something to do with it. Or is it simply a preparation of myself to face it and handle it successfully? I don't think I can live one day at a time. Yesterday is gone, but I had a part to play in it. Today is here, and I am working on it. Tomorrow is in God's hands, being prepared for me. I eagerly reach out for it and will work it into the tapestry of my life in anticipation of the next tomorrow that God is working on for me.

In this manner life does have meaning, and my todays are not horrible moments to be lived through blindly in fear and anxiety. I cannot do this alone, but in harmony with God there is meaning to the moment and raison d'être in the day-by-day happenings.

I need a hand in shaping my destiny; I am not the plaything of fate. I am in the hands of a loving God, who cares and controls and heals. Nothing is going to happen to me outside His will. This way even death is cheated out of its victory, and the sting is resolved into a sweet affirmation of peace.

Testings? Is God testing His strength in my frail faith and frame? If this be the case, it will be made perfect in my weakness, and in this strength (His strength) we can conquer today and tomorrow and bury our yesterdays in His eternity. My security is in His keeping—and it makes the difference.

Monday, July 16

Back in the lineup again. So routine, so impersonal, yet so together. Some have completed their therapy, and new ones are taking their places. On and on and on we go with that curse of humanity—CANCER! Will it never be defeated?

I feel like crying out, "How did you feel when you learned . . . ?" Such absolute despondency and anger in the lineup this morning.

"Rev. S., you can 'come in' now . . ." When I "come out," voices (some hardly audible) respond, "See you tomorrow . . . good luck." I wave and try to smile. I'm dizzy; my stomach crawls. I hang on to the rail along the wall and try to assure them, "It's going to be OK!" A friend of mine used to call it, "Whistling by the graveyard." And sometimes I feel like that is exactly what I am trying to do.

Trying to hide fears, anxieties, and offer courage to others. Is it just a game? Sometimes the reality seems too much. And I ask myself, "Is this God's healing process? Do I have to die before I can live? Is He mocking my fears?" But then a faith works up through the surface, and I try to smile and believe even while it is hurting.

What's happening, God? What are You trying to teach me? Hold me steady! Then I walk out on Tremont Street and stumble up to the subway, and I meet another world—other

75

people who are waiting for the verdict and for "The Machine." And I try to walk straight and forget, and I hide the hurt from others. I have to act like everybody else. Rushing. Rushing. Rushing.

Then I ask, "Is everybody else hurting somewhere inside? Are you hiding your hurts too? Let us talk about them together." But everybody rushes on. Afraid. Hurting. Reaching.

Tuesday, July 17

Fred went with me today. Tried to act very brave, but so dazed that I stumbled down the steps at Park Street and walked into a glass wall at Brighams. Other problems arise too great to handle at this time.

Vacation plans to be made. Hurt too much to think rationally. I can suffer this out alone. God help me not to go off the deep end but find some meaning for which all this is taking place.

I am going to bed and leave it in the care of One who can work it all out. I sure can't.

Wednesday, July 18

Got through the ordeal today and went to prayer meeting tonight. Got backed into a corner by a Job's comforter. He spent an overextended amount of time airing a philosophy of life for one in the midst of a cancer concern. He must have been reading Kubler-Ross.

"You go through three stages—at first you feel bad. Then you realize that the thing has got you, and you get mad and say, 'What's the use?' and drive on. Here comes a loss of hope, and defiance spells the difference between defeat or victory. There is a firm grasp now for survival that knocks resignation out of the way." And on and on he went, and I found the counsel as bad as the cancer. But maybe I am learning something here for future use!

Thursday, July 19

Calls today. Glen from Halifax. Art from Montreal. Paul from Hanson. "Hope you will be able to make it to camp." They keep in touch with love and concern. How can I let them down?

Monday, July 23

Boston as usual. Early treatment. Not as bad as before. Sat on my "own" park bench on the Common and watched the world writhe and struggle in their hurts and dilemmas.

Ambulance came and picked up a young man who had been "out" on the grass since yesterday morning.

Young, bearded, disheveled man came by and asked for money, while a woman on the bench across the walk asked, "Say, mister, have you got a cigarette?" Began conversation with her. Husband died an alcoholic. Son in medical school. She lives alone but comes to the Common every day with her bottle and smokes and drinks and "makes a living."

Recognizes that it is the wrong way to live, but has been in this routine so long that she can't break herself away. She used to go to church, "but they drink too, and I am as good as they are." Oh, this hurting humanity living in a world that doesn't care. Where have we failed them?

The Common is a perfect place for a ministry to people who have lost the way. There must be a diamond in the debris out there somewhere. The devil does not let them off easily. She responded to every overture of concern with those words of finality, "I'm a lost cause."

Thursday, July 26

Last treatment. I'm tired. I'm sick. This thing is going to kill me yet!

Summary

The doctor shook my hand and said, "Well, Reverend, it's over." Inside I asked, "What's over? Your part of the ordeal? Where do I stand?"

"We all have cancer. We have a minister with us, and he has cancer too. Maybe he will pray for us."

Guess I haven't handled this thing too well, and I am not proud of my journey. Sometimes I get angry and am ready to chuck it all, and sometimes I tell God just how mean He has treated me. And I am surprised that He takes it all and doesn't turn His back on me. Looking back over this ordeal, I haven't given Him much to build His kingdom on. I have fought hard for that inner strength that would ultimately pull me through. I have cried and complained, and I have argued and kicked, and often my faith was running on a very thin edge.

I used to preach to my people to look at the difficulties of the present as momentary. That old adage, "For this, too, shall pass away," for the strength upon which they could rest was nothing less than the omnipotence of God, and they could depend on Him.

Sounded good! But, preacher, you have never been herded in a therapy stall like a bunch of cattle that have been branded for death by cancer, where the mood swings from anger to frustration and fear and accusation and pity.

Where can one find dignity, much less peace, in the midst of such vexation and difficulties? Where is the assurance that all this torment can be but for the moment? How do I know that this suffering is not lost in the hands of violence and death? My life is threatened. And the finger of truth and hope point to me, "You've got cancer?" "We have a minister here, and he has cancer, too. Let's ask him to pray for us." And the mockery stabs to the very depth of the soul. And I cringe, and I hurt, and I get frustrated, and I accuse!

And I asked, "Why?"

And God answered, "Because!"

And in His "because" I learned that only a face-to-face confrontation with Him can mitigate fears in the crisis of death, and that there are prayers that only He can hear. The dilemma recognizes our weakness and our littleness, but it also recognizes God's eternality. He knows the hurt and the frustration we have to endure, and He has written down the answer to every question.

I learned that you can speak the deepest secrets of the soul and reveal your most solemn thoughts to God, and you will not be ridiculed, nor will He trample your fears and questions under His feet.

Then I am reminded of the day that little Jimmie came to play with Grandpa. He was sick and felt more like staying in bed, but he did not want to disappoint me. He crawled up on my lap, put his little arms around my neck, and asked, "Grandpa Ken, do you still love me when I'm sick?"

Then the instant replay of the past few months with the anxiety and pain and the fear and questions began to roll by in full review, and I heard God say, "When you fuss and question and cry and get discouraged and throw in the towel, and when you get sick, I know all about it—and I do still love you."

Then He asks, "How far down the road did I tell you that you could see, anyway?" And there comes that faith that just won't let you go. Whatever may be the difficulties (cancer, therapy, loss of health, bills, etc.), you sense that God knew all about them from the beginning and has them all under control.

Guess I don't have much to do with the road, or the hills, or the valleys; but "I . . . am persuaded that he is able to keep that which I have committed unto him against that day" (2 Tim. 1:12), and that "neither death, nor life . . . shall be able to separate us from the love of God, which is in Christ Jesus our Lord" (Rom. 8:38-39).

Today, July 26, 1984, I will trust Him for His healing, if it is His will. As for the resources that are required—they, too, are hidden in His omnipotence!

NOTE: September 1987. After a series of tests, X rays, and scans the conclusion of the doctor after reading the reports was, "Well, it looks like you have been cured; there are no signs of cancer cells."

Prayers for Pastoral Ministry
and
Personal Meditation

*

AFFLICTION

You have smoothed out our beds for us, O God, in our affliction and given us rest in our souls and reminded us that our bodies are the temples of the Holy Spirit. You have satisfied our hunger and have drawn water for us when the well was too deep and we had nothing with which to draw. You have quenched our thirst and satisfied our minds and hearts that we may be in fellowship with You at the throne of grace. Help us to understand the purposes of God; then the night shall be full of stars, and the daybreak shall be the beginning of heaven.*

*

Stand by us when we have to carry great weights beyond our strength. Make our beds for us when the day is spent. Touch our bread when it is coming down to the last crust of the loaf, that we might have more at the end than at the beginning. Deal with our enemies that we might not see them because of Your nearness; do not destroy them, but turn them into friends of God. In Jesus' name we pray.

ANGUISH

Help that one who has fallen back into sin and reaches

81

out for that which is wholly forbidden. Oh, the tortures of this wild contradiction! They are mad with anguish almost too much to bear. Their cheeks burn with shame hotter than fire. They would that Lazarus be sent with some cooling water to ease the infinite torment, but no human answer comes to the crying of the pain. With You, O God, are all the mercies of the Cross. Only as men cry out to You, "God be merciful to me a sinner," does the sweet peace come following divine pardon!

*

Thank You, Lord, for the measure of comfort You bring in laying before us the highest truths of Your ministry. Often we search heaven and earth in our anguish for effective ways for the triumph of our faith. How simply Jesus comes to us in telling us that He is Bread, He is Water, He is Light, He is the Door, and He is the Shepherd. These words, so simple, stretch their meaning around the whole circle of our searching. O Jesus, You do not liken yourself to the luxuries and heavy understanding of life but to the necessities. We need You, blessed Jesus, as a necessity and not as a luxury. Come to us, we pray, as Bread and Water and the Answer to the real needs of our soul. In Your name we pray. Amen.

BEREAVEMENT

Almighty God, we pray that You will help the bereaved ones to bear the loss that has so recently come into the home. Give them light even in the dark hours and in the dreariest of silence. May they hear a voice speaking to the heart. The loss may come, and how helpless we are to hinder it, but do not close Your ears to the midnight cry. And on those tired eyes gently lay the tender touch of slumber. So often we weep and wonder and worry; but then comes a voice of assurance and whispers, "It is better for those who have gone, for they have gone forward to the coronation!" We remain to plow and sow in all the foul winds and weather, in all tumults and uproars, and bear the sting of life's keen pains. While we do not understand it all, give us faith to know that in the moment of deepest heartache God has promised to give the oil of joy for mourning. For this we are thankful!

*

There are many hurting hearts in our world today, God, who have been bereaved or are in circumstances of special distress. Out of Your tender, compassionate heart send angels from heaven who will speak to them of Your care, love, and wisdom. Show them, O merciful Father, that even in the darkest hours there is meaning in all the chastening providences of life.

BROKEN HEARTS

We pray for the brokenhearted and many who are carrying the hurt under the cloak of laughter. Theirs are shattered lives that never tell the whole story of their ruin, and they guard the truth and hurt as a great secret. They long for God but don't dare to make the longing known before a critical and unjust world. But You know every desire, O God, and every ambition and purpose that frustrates and burns with unquenchable fire. Create in each broken heart Your own purpose, through Your Holy Spirit, and fashion each one to Your own will; then use each one to Your own glory!

*

How the great heart of God is moved over the broken heart, the eyes that are filled with burning tears, and the penitent sinner crying for mercy at the foot of the Cross. This is Your majestic moment, O God! This is Your finest hour! Heaven is hushed in silence when the brokenhearted cry for mercy. I cried unto the Lord from the deep pit. He heard my cry. He lifted me out. Hallelujah!

BURDENS

O God, help us carry life's burdens with some measure of cheerfulness. May we ever be able to say, "This also cometh from the Lord." Give us the faith to believe that You are aware of all the things that come into our lives and that You care and are willing to stay close beside us through all the difficulties.

—Often there is a great cross.
—Often we are under a heavy cloud.
—Often we face a tremendous loss.
—Often we meet with weakening infirmities.
—Often we meet for the first time an aging body.

Then we can count the stones along the road as jewels, and the cross will be the way to the crown. In all of life's perplexities may we see them as disciplines that will have as their promises exceeding great rewards.

*

O God, we pray that Your grace and enduring love will accompany us to the end of time. There are burdens to carry down here, and sorrows for which we have no interpretation except that it is the will of God. There will be many tears to shed that are not in our planning. But these things are just for the nighttime, for we have been assured that joy comes singing in the morning. When the end comes, it will not be an ending but just the beginning—the opening to a brighter world. And how beautiful heaven must be!

COMPASSION

Almighty God, You have given us comfort by Your grace and healed us from the awful leprosy of sin that was eating our soul away. Abundantly You come to us in the mercies of every day. Because Your compassions do not fail, You have spared us to this moment. We are monuments of mercy, witnesses of grace, miracles of the love of God, and overwhelmed by Your love for Your people. You have given us ready answers for the difficult time, and You have taken the sword from the enemy. May our prayer be richer, our service be truer, and our hands be quick to do Your bidding.

∗

O God, Yours is a kind eye, a tender look, a heart of pity—Your mercy endures forever. When our father's pity fails and there is no more love in our mother's heart, Your abundant mercy has just begun. There is no measure to it, and no line can be laid upon it, and no man has found the shore of this great sea. We know these things, for we live every day in Your mercy. If Your pity were less, our life would be shorter. Because Your compassion fails not, our days run on. We live and move and have our being in Your unwasting love. Glory!

CONFUSION

O God, how a little shining of light from heaven makes us glad! It is a foretaste of a time of peace and rest and joy. You have put within our week a day on which there shall be a proclamation of mercy and sympathy and love. And on that day that is set aside for the worship of God some hint of life's great meaning shall shine in the hearts of His people. And we pray that Your sun shall write the answer of light upon every mystery that has troubled the mind and heart, and give each one peace in the midst of so much confusion.

∗

Because You are holy, O God, we are afraid; but because You are love, we take heart again, and through this love we find our way through great confusion to Your holiness. We have no answer to this, and we have no defense of ourselves against Your righteousness. But when You bend yourself in tender love, and when we feel Your teardrop on us in pity, we find the sweet assurance that even we, though chief of sinners, can obtain pardon at the Cross. Then the day dawns and the summer wind breathes upon us, and we feel all heaven coming down with glad welcomes and certainty of infinite salvation and adoption into the holiness of heaven. This experience we now enjoy, for it brings peace when uncertainty and confusion would reign.

DEATH

Almighty God, our hearts are full of fear as we think about dying; teach us the true meaning of death. We know that we all must die, but give us the assurance that even though we die, by being in Christ we shall die into a greater life. Help us to know that we do not die into darkness and extinction, but we die into light and immortality. Jesus Christ brought this great truth to our attention in His Gospels to us. Now we can say, "O death, where is thy sting? O grave, where is thy victory?" We triumph in the Lord's victory; we rise again in His resurrection!

*

O God, there has been no death that has left such an impact on humanity as we have witnessed on the hill outside the city of Jerusalem.

—We saw Him going to His death!
—We saw Him carrying His own heavy cross.
—We watched as they nailed His hands and feet to that awful tree.
—We saw the Son of God in His last agony in love on earth.
—We heard the cry of victory reverberate again and again around the world.

We asked the questions, "Why this uplifted Cross?" "Why the cry of pain and separation?" "Why the darkness and all the wonders that accompanied the Crucifixion?" Then we saw it

86

written by the finger of eternity, even as the stars are placed by the hand of divinity: "For God so loved the world, that he gave his only begotten Son, that whosoever believeth in him should not perish, but have everlasting life." This is heaven's explanation to the ages, world without end. It satisfies the imagination and brings comfort to the soul. It reconciles all nature to God—and we are part of the plan. Hallelujah!

DELIVERANCE

Deliver us, O God, from vain ideas and impulses that would extend our boundaries and promote our influences in our own name and strength. Help us to know that only by the good name of God can we conquer and set our achievements among our victories in Him.

*

"Lead us not into temptation, but deliver us from evil"— the words of the Master to His disciples. After we have been delivered, we pray that we may be established in all goodness and in the love of truth. This we know we can do only in the power of Christ and for the sake of Christ who died for us. The Cross is our surety, our refuge, and the answer to our being delivered from the binding chains of iniquity. At the Cross we are happy to leave every prayer.

DISAPPOINTMENT

O God, You have never disappointed the honest heart seeking after You. The soul whose burning desire is to find God has always been gratified by a revelation of Your presence. Increase our faith, O Lord, as we seek after You. Help us rid ourselves of the petty notions that deceive and mock us every day. We would live in the Spirit, walking and talking and communing with God. Create this desire within by Your blessed Holy Spirit—the Gift of the cross of Christ. Then will our past become greater and our future brighter if our present can rest in the security of the Cross.

*

We thank You, O God, for life, notwithstanding its pain, its shadows, and its disappointments. It is a daily struggle with death, and in its most beauteous aspects it runs along the valley, which is full of graves. Yet life is a great privilege, a keen joy, and a challenge to become enlarged in experience, ennobled in character, and glorified in eternity. Help us to receive life in this spirit. And when we are stung by its pain and grieved by its disappointments, may we rest our little griefs upon the infinite sorrow of the Son of God.

ENCOURAGEMENT

In great despair, O God, we could have been brought to our knees before the holiness of God. Yet You have spared us the shame of our ways and brought great encouragement instead of a sudden avalanche of woe. So great is Your love and so all-forgiving is Your spirit that we can come without defense or excuse. In our faraway wondering and obstinacy of heart You have sent Your Holy Spirit with Your message that the door is still open and that Christ is mighty to redeem.

*

Help us, O God, not to look to other sources for our strength, our encouragement, and our sustenance. Let the Cross be the object of our love and the kingdom of Christ the supreme hope of our life. Encourage us in our bewilderment and in our longing for release and light upon our way. Keep us steady in the things we have to do, and help us not to relax our hold upon the plow until the going down of the sun. Let a bit of heaven descend upon our soul so that we may overhear its music and rejoice by the encouragement of its ineffable rest.

FORSAKEN

We praise You, O God, with a loud voice and a cheerful

heart, because Your gifts are many, Your love is constant, and Your mercy is very tender. You do not forsake that one for whom Calvary's blood was poured out. We are often walking under the clouds, but even there Your voice comes to us, saying, "This is my beloved Son: hear him"; You did not forsake Him. When the clouds have passed away, we see no man save Jesus only, and our hearts are completely satisfied.

*

Forsaken! How ugly a thought to enter into the human mind. May our souls never have to know the reality of this tremendous sentence of heaven! We would ever stand before God's face and be blessed with the light of His benediction. We would be inspired and comforted by all the tenderness of His great heart. This desire rests in our hearts with the knowledge that we have not been forsaken. As you make the fruit to grow in abundance on the trees of the field, so make the human heart to respond to all the goodness of heaven. Draw us closer to the bleeding side as You enclose us with Your arms of love.

HEALING

We want to give ourselves more perfectly to You, O God. So we pray for Your healing—full, radiant, and abounding. May the mind be strong and every nerve respond to the working of an able body. Thus in great health of body may we entertain a healthy, loving soul. Take away all diseases, all infirmity and imperfections with every sign and token of death. And may we trample death in the dust while we live on in vigor and happiness. You know the meaning of our prayer, though we cannot utter the words as we would like. Look not on our words but on our thoughts, and lengthen our days in valuable service to God.

*

O God, we make the Cross our meeting place. For here is where heaven begins, because Christ died here for the lost man and woman, and here He sealed the pardon of a believing world. How can we thank You, O God, for the Cross? It meets all of our necessities, and it answers all the cry and pain and gives health to the sin-sick soul. In the Cross is the Balm of healing that can be found in no other place. May we ever live at the Cross. Then the crown will be assured, and all heaven will welcome those whose love is secure in the Son of God.

IMMORTALITY

Almighty God, we continually look for the Lord Jesus, who will someday change our body and make it like His glorious body. When our citizenship is complete in heaven, we shall walk with the saints in the light and do Thy will without weariness. This anticipation makes us strong, so that the valley is as the mountain and the rough places as a road smoothed by God. These are the miracles that God works in our experience, so that we need have no fear of time and space and sense and limitation. But we act and move and work with God in control in those uppermost places where the light never fades.

*

O God, we pray that we might get a vision of the immortality of the Almighty. We know that this is too great a thing to ask; so may we look upon Your goodness, for we know that we cannot bear the luster of Your glory and still live. We thank You for all light, truth, peace, and hope, which are the gifts of God. Every day You enrich our lives with these as You give us the promise of life and take away the fear of death. This is the great gospel of Jesus Christ. This is life and immortality and heaven, for living in Your light we can never die. Oh, the mystery of love and the marvel of continual grace found in the love of Jesus Christ!

90

MOURNING

Almighty God, because You love us, You turn our mourning into joy, and You make our tears a blessing. You abolish death and set the grave on the road to heaven and soothe the aching heart with the balm of Your presence. All of this You do in Jesus Christ, Your dear Son, our one and only Savior. How infinite in His sufficiency, tender beyond all human love, and inexhaustible in His compassion. Blessed are those who mourn and who have this hope!

*

"Blessed are the dead which die in the Lord." But those who are left behind need comfort for the loss so recently suffered. We pray, O God, that You will bring a sense of Your purpose and presence to that one who has felt the cold chill of death move in. Speak tenderly to those where the encroachment of the graveyard has threatened their household. Show the mourning ones that their hope is from above and that their home is on high, for here we have no continuing city, but that our permanence is beyond the clouds.

TENDERNESS

O God, we know about Your great mercy through Your grace, and we stand amazed at Your tenderness through Your love. All history testifies to the fact that Your mercy endures forever. We are glad and astonished with an infinite astonishment because our God is pitiful and His eyes are full of tears while His heart melts with tenderness. How often, O God, You lift the thunder, lest the poor victim should be crushed never to rise again. You take the sting of pain out of the heart, and in our mouth You put a new and living song. Continue to comfort, we pray, all the way through the wilderness with the assurance of Your enduring mercy so that our lives shall be an eternal testimony to Your grace.

*

Our only hope, O God, is in Your love. And this love we know best in Jesus Christ, the Priest, the Offering for our sins and, thank God, the sins of the whole world. And in this love we meet the Father. It is God's own love—eternal, unchangeable, infinite. We hide ourselves in it as in a sanctuary of tenderness that cannot be violated. Here we stand in this infinite enclosure, safe from attack and guarded against every subtle temptation of the enemy. In Your tenderness is Your love, and in Your love is our refuge.

TROUBLE

There are shadows and troubles in every life, O God, and some today are breathing prayers in secret that they dare not and cannot put in words. Hear their sighing and withdraw the thorn that has wounded the heart to its innermost fiber. Let them find new supplies of grace, and surprise them with new and sudden incoming light. Show them that even yet there is meal in the barrel and oil in the cruse. While they seek these things, help them grow under the strong arm of faith. Destroy the spirit of fear, for it is a destroyer of faith; and give us that perfect love that casts out fear. Then when troubles come, our faith will overcome, and our fears will disappear as the dew before the burning sun of summer.

*

Almighty God, help us not to think of the troubles we have had to pass through, for the joy of victory in God is greater because of the sorrow. We forget the night when morning has dawned, as the reaper forgets the seedtime in the day of golden harvest when the barns are too small and the fields are rich with grain. So we forget our troubles in the moment of gladness. Trouble is but for a moment, but joy is an exceeding great and eternal weight of glory!

UNDERSTANDING

Almighty God, we earnestly pray that You will give us the hearing ear and the understanding heart so that not one word of all Your law will be lost upon us.

—Open our eyes that we may see the wonderful things out of Your law.

—Open our understanding so that we may know more of Your holy Scriptures.

—May the Holy Spirit inspire us to know the meaning of God's law and God's love.

—May the Book reveal the living Spirit and bring us into harmony with all His purposes.

—Help us, by faith, to lay hold of the words of love and live upon them.

To this end we pray for a double portion of the Holy Spirit as we say, "Speak, Lord; for thy servant heareth."

*

Dry our tears when we are hard pressed by difficulty and storm and heavy laden with grief. Give us sleep at the end of the day and help us forget our woe and gain back our strength. May we begin each day's battle with all the hopefulness of renewed energy. We can ask all these things because of a God of love who understands and cares.

*

Save us, O God, from self-delusion and self-defeat. May we understand ourselves, knowing what strength we have and by what weakness we are rendered helpless. Then help us understand how near God is to supply our needs according to His riches in glory by Christ Jesus, our Lord! May the life of Your Son be a new life and challenge to Your people everywhere. May a new mystery of unity show itself day by day as we throw ourselves in complete faith upon the infinite heart of Your love. In Jesus' name we pray. AMEN!

*These prayers are based, in part, on *The People's Bible,* by Joseph Parker.

Bibliography

Becker, Ernest. 1973. *The Denial of Death.* New York: Free Press.

Giovacchine, Peter, M.D. 1981. *The Urge to Die.* New York: Macmillan Publishing Co.

Irion, Paul E. 1954. *The Funeral and the Mourners.* New York: Abingdon Press.

Kastenbaum, Robert, and Aisenberg, Ruth. 1976. *The Psychology of Death.* New York: Springer Publishing Co.

Kubler-Ross, Elisabeth. 1969. *On Death and Dying.* New York: Macmillan Publishing Co.

———. 1975. *Death: The Final Stage of Growth.* Englewood Cliffs, N.J.: Prentice-Hall.

Matthews, Joseph W. 1964. *Motive,* January-February. Nashville.

Parker, Joseph. 1887. *The People's Bible.* New York: Funk and Wagnalls.

Rogers, William. 1950. *Ye Shall Be Comforted.* Philadelphia: Westminster Press.

Schultz, Richard. 1978. *The Psychology of Death, Dying, and Bereavement.* Reading, Mass.: Addison-Wesley Publishing Co.

Singler, Lawrence J. "The Slowly Dying Child."

Tillich, Paul. 1948. *The Shaking of the Foundations.* New York: Charles Scribner's Sons.

Wynn, John Charles. 1957. *Pastoral Ministries to Families.* Philadelphia: Westminster Press.

Zeller, William W. "Values in Sickness and Health."